MISSION-CENTERED
— *Apologetics* —

*Demolishing Intellectual Stumbling Blocks
and Declaring the Truth of the Gospel*

DON McINTOSH

Mission-Centered Apologetics:
Demolishing Intellectual Stumbling Blocks
and Declaring the Truth of the Gospel

Copyright © 2020 by Don McIntosh.

Gerizim Publishing
San Antonio, Texas
www.gerizimpublishing.com

ISBN: 978-0-578-64764-7

Cover inset illustration by Pixabay. Used by permission.

All rights reserved. No part of this publication may be reproduced, stored in a retrieval system, or transmitted, in any form or by any means, electronic, mechanical, photocopying, recording or otherwise without the permission of the author.

Unless otherwise noted, Scripture references are from the New King James Version of the Holy Bible. Copyright © 1982, Thomas Nelson, Inc. Used by permission. All rights reserved.

*Dedicated to all the churches of the saints,
especially these:*

The Association of Vineyard Churches

The Foursquare Church

Christian Fellowship Ministries

CONTENTS

Preface	7
1. Introduction: Apologetics in the Mission of the Church	11
2. Evil and the Problem of Suffering	23
3. Evidence and the Burden of Proof	43
4. Evolution, Science, and Technology	57
5. Exclusivism and the Claims of Christ	79
Postscript: Revisiting Pascal's Wager	87
Endnotes	91

PREFACE

My conversion to Christianity is easily the greatest thing that ever happened to me. When I first put my trust in Christ in the Fall of 1985, thirty-five years ago, I was immediately – as C.S. Lewis put it famously – "surprised by joy." I was delivered from long-standing sinful habits, deep guilt and shame, and a certain discontented restlessness that no amount of activity, revelry or self-indulgence could seem to cure. I realized at once why I was born into the world. I had found the "pearl of great price," the "hidden treasure," which Jesus spoke of in his parables: the kingdom of God, supernaturally ruled by a great and gracious King, Jesus Christ himself.

Not long after my conversion, however, I came across questions that troubled me. I was a student at the University of Texas, and for the coming Spring semester I had registered for courses in evolutionary biology, astronomy, and eighteenth-century philosophy. A new and relatively naïve believer like me could not have asked for a more faith-challenging curriculum. The question of creation and evolution in biology was the first to confront me, and the one that impacted me most powerfully. But there were other questions, about the origin of the universe, about miracles and the laws of nature, and indeed about whether there was any room at all for a loving, all-powerful God in a rational view of the world. These questions shook me, so much that

Mission-Centered Apologetics

I briefly lost my faith and became something like a religious agnostic. By that I mean that I was still gathering with believers at church, reading my Bible and praying, but all the while full of doubts.

Not willing to drop my faith completely without studying it out a little further, I began to spend all my spare time holed up in the university library, reading relevant books, exploring the issues from all sides, and taking lots of notes. Gradually, a different, more intellectually rigorous view of the faith took hold in my mind. I came away from that experience blurry-eyed but convinced that even if some questions remained, most of the criticisms of my faith were greatly overblown. I also came away angry and disappointed with my professors, most of whom I suspected were familiar enough with arguments from the other side but deliberately kept them from their students.

Ever since that time I have maintained an interest in apologetics. Although I no longer struggle with such doubts the way I once did, I continue to engage in apologetics as a ministry to skeptically minded people. Not only university students, but people from all walks of life often stand in need of a reason to believe. Simply enduring the bewildering, tragic circumstances of life can rattle one's faith in God. Beyond that, there is a subtle but certain stigma often implicitly associated with genuine commitment to Jesus Christ, along with a tendency in our modernized, highly developed society to glorify science and technology at the expense of faith. All this is good reason for Christians to learn and understand apologetics, and defend the integrity of the faith when and where necessary.

Preface

But right here I have to throw in a caveat; for in recent years apologetics seems to have taken on a life of its own, and become almost as much an *industry* as a ministry. Indeed, one may wonder why someone like me would bother with another book on apologetics, given that a search for "apologetics" in the Books category at Amazon.com yields over 10,000 titles. Today there are seemingly hundreds of professional apologists hosting extensive apologetic ministries, of which I would guess there were less than a couple of dozen back when I first came into the faith. Their purpose, moreover, often appears to be *strictly* apologetic, that is, not related to any larger missional or evangelistic effort. I see lots of arguments for the intellectual truth of the gospel; I see comparatively few appeals to repent and believe that gospel.

One inspiration (or *provocation*, really) for writing this book was something I came across on Twitter a couple of years ago: a "March Madness" apologetics competition, complete with a 64-competitor bracket and head-to-head "matchups" between well-known apologists, for which Christians with a Twitter account could vote. Maybe I'm just envious because I've been publicly involved in apologetics for over thirty years and didn't make the cut – but honestly, this seems misguided. Even if it's said to be "all in fun," a public contest like this seems to send the wrong message. I would say the same if the purpose of the contest were instead to crown the best pastor, best scholar, most anointed worship leader, most accurate prophet, most insightful teacher, or most productive soul-winning evangelist. Whenever we find ourselves trying to determine who is "greatest in the kingdom," I suspect we have begun to lose our way.

The mission to which Jesus calls us is not to make a buck or make a name for ourselves. It is to make disciples of all the nations. I write in the hope not only that Christians learn apologetics, but also that we can learn to redirect our apologetic efforts towards the spiritual needs of the harvest in these last days.

Don McIntosh
San Antonio, Texas

1. INTRODUCTION: APOLOGETICS IN THE MISSION OF THE CHURCH

I am a Christian today for many reasons. I love God and believe in him with all my heart. I appreciate the ministry of Jesus and the salvation he promises: forgiveness of sins and new life in his everlasting kingdom. When I read the words of Jesus, those words ring not only true, but with authority. I believe that anyone who sincerely puts their trust in Jesus Christ is morally and spiritually better off for it, and that Christianity generally makes the world a happier, better place. I have lots of good Christian friends and meaningful Christian connections. Besides all that, I have already been a dedicated Christian believer myself for some thirty-five years and it's been a blessing to me so far. These all seem to be pretty good reasons for me to be a Christian.

One reason stands well above all the others, however, and that reason is that I believe the Christian message is *true* – that it corresponds to reality. The way I see it, if Christianity is *not* true, then none of the other reasons for believing in Christ can really be justified. While it cannot be denied that the gospel promises (and delivers!) personal transformation, new life, joy, peace, and untold other spiritual benefits, these more subjective realities are always and ultimately founded on the basic fact that the Christian faith is objectively true. To take Paul's doctrine of justification by faith a step further: if the believer is justified by faith, that faith is justified in turn by the gospel being true. Paul himself seemed to feel the same way, going so far as to say that if Christ is not truly, bodily, physically risen from the dead, then the Christian faith is "futile" (or "useless" or "worthless," 1 Cor. 15:17).

Among the various propositions Christians claim to be objectively true are these: (1) God, the omnipotent creator of the universe, exists; (2) God has made his existence evident to all men through the visible witness of the creation and the invisible witness of his moral nature written on the conscience; (3) God has further made his existence evident through a series of personal revelations and interventions in history, from the call of Abraham, to the Exodus led by Moses, to the judgments and prognostications of the prophets, to the miraculous ministry and sacrificial, atoning death of Jesus; and (4) God has demonstrated and vindicated the saving ministry of Jesus by raising him from the dead.

What all this indicates is that Christianity is not merely a well-established major religion, an insightful philosophical position, or the single greatest cultural source of moral teachings or spiritual inspiration, but a universal truth claim. That is, either Christianity is true or it is false. And if it is true, it is true for everyone in the world. And if it is true for everyone in the world, then those of us who know it to be true are obligated to let the rest of the world know as well. In other words there are good reasons for *everyone*, not just me, to believe in Christ.

Introduction

This connection between truth and mission was not lost on Jesus' disciples. The earliest apostles came to believe that Jesus held out the hope of eternal life, that he died for the sins of the world, that he had risen from the dead to publicly confirm his message, and finally, that he had appeared to them personally after his resurrection. Because they believed certain basic propositions to be *true*, they not only remained true to the faith themselves but were willing to answer and obey the Great Commission of Christ, to preach the gospel to all the world and make disciples of all the nations.

The Call to Engage in Apologetics

Now clearly not everyone who hears the message of Christianity believes it to be true. As Christians on mission, then, we can respond in one of two ways when confronted with unbelief: (1) reason with the nonbeliever in an effort to inspire faith and conversion; or (2) walk away from the nonbeliever and move on to more promising conversion prospects. The first option requires engagement in Christian *apologetics*, which means to present an *apologia* or "defense" of the faith – to present reasons for the nonbeliever to believe. The second option takes a more businesslike approach to the mission field, in which individual nonbelievers are not permitted to get in the way of maximizing returns on the evangelistic investment in terms of number of recorded conversions.

While each of these options may be valid, depending on the particular audience in question, I believe the love of God would require us to make at least an initial, serious apologetic effort to convince nonbelieving hearers of the truth of the gospel. At the same time, I believe Christians on mission must be careful to *stay* on mission and "beware," as Paul said, of intellectual and philosophical diversions that lead to nothing but strife. Unfortunately, the church appears to have dropped the ball on both counts. Entire apologetics "ministries" have sprung up dedicated to nothing but contentious arguments, often technical to the point of public inaccessibility and often presented with the implicit, even explicit, purpose of embarrassing skeptics and critics. Meanwhile, well-meaning evangelists concerned to win large numbers of souls claim to have "no time" for intellectual questions, since such questions presumably reflect a "proud heart" or an "independent spirit" – as if Jesus died for all sins except those.

First Peter 3:15 has long been considered the classic text on apologetics: "But sanctify the Lord God in your hearts, and always be ready to give a defense to everyone who asks you a reason for the hope that is in you, with meekness and fear." Two words in particular give this verse apologetic significance: "defense," derived from *apologia* (ἀπολογία) in the Greek, and "reason" or *logos* (λόγος). But apparently more emphasis needs to be given to the call for ministering with "meekness and fear." Peter adds this caution, I believe, because the very act of arguing lends itself naturally to strife, pride and intellectual arrogance. As a practicing apologist-evangelist myself, I am well aware of just how easy it is to slip into highly personal, peevish disputations far removed from any concern for the salvation of souls or the glory of God – a situation made that

Introduction

much worse when the argument takes place in full public view.

Many years ago while first learning the ropes doing apologetics on the Internet, I wrote up what I called "Don's Rules for Apologetic Discourse." Since I believe these are still relevant and still important, I will share them here:

1. *Be respectful.* Men are made in the image of God, and Jesus died for every one of them. Skeptics do not necessarily even believe in "love" per se, but they do generally respond well to overtures of respect. That means, among other things, acknowledging valid points, passing up opportunities for insults, and refusing to gloat over your own perceived victories.

2. *Be honest.* Vocal unbelievers are usually well-educated, especially in the natural sciences, and once in a while they may catch you in an error or misstatement of fact. If you find yourself in the wrong, you'll retain more credibility if you swallow your pride and concede to the facts. In this way, you can exhibit some genuine humility and learn something new at the same time. I believe it was A.J. Toynbee who said, "The only purpose for debates is to learn. Or at least it's the only purpose that makes any sense."

3. *Be original.* Many members of the skeptical community are well-versed in C.S. Lewis and Josh McDowell, but they've probably never heard of

Mission-Centered Apologetics

you. Tell them what you think; you may surprise them with a carefully thought out response of your own.

4. *Pay attention*. Likewise, freethinking unbelievers may have something to say that you haven't read in a primer on apologetics. A well rehearsed knee-jerk response is not always appropriate, nor even relevant to what was said.

5. *Do your homework*. Find out what the leading intellectuals are saying. If atheists keep bringing up Richard Dawkins' theory of cumulative natural selection or Stephen Hawking's take on the strong anthropic principle, read up on it. Learn the basics of logic and logical fallacies. Try not to contradict yourself or circumvent the real issues.

6. *Remember your audience*. One irrational, overly antagonistic critic won't spoil the whole bunch. Chances are good that other people – unbelievers leaning toward faith and believers struggling with doubts – will be looking on with interest. Socrates never taught the proud, aggressive Thrasymachus much of anything, but in debating Thrasymachus he revealed many truths to many others.

It's clear to me now that one important rule was missing from my list:

7. *Remember your mission*.

Introduction

I add that last one because apologetics, though often interesting and even fascinating, is not an end in itself. There comes a point in every apologetic encounter when the argument either makes its mark or becomes unfruitful. As Paul suggested in various places, the tendency beyond that point is to wrangle: to argue about the meanings of words, the strength or validity of the arguments themselves, even the sincerity and motives of our "opponents" – the very people we have been called to reach. The gospel quickly gets lost in the exchange, and Christians, if we are not careful, can begin to see people as enemies to be defeated rather than precious souls to be won.

One purpose of this little book is to train Christian evangelists to walk a narrow path. That path is marked by an appeal to dialogue with nonbelievers using knowledge, reason, compassion and humility on one side; and by the larger, looming, ever-present, ever-pressing mission to win the world for Christ on the other. Jesus called his disciples, and all Christians by implication, to be "fishers of men." Certain kinds of fish that gather in schools are best caught by casting a wide net over the water. But if we are to be effective fishermen, we must also learn how to catch other kinds of fish using specific lures. Apologetics is one of those lures. If apologetics helps to bring my neighbor Bob to faith in Christ, then I would be wise to continue using apologetics with people like Bob. If apologetics does *not* work with Bob, then I should try a different lure. And if other lures do not work, only then should I consider leaving Bob to himself and fishing elsewhere.

Intellectual Stumbling Blocks

Scripture often mentions "stumbling blocks." These are issues, circumstances, or even people, that make faith exceedingly difficult – like a hurdle that's too high to clear. Paul mentions in First Corinthians for example that the message of Christ crucified for our sins is "to the Jews a stumbling block" (2:23). Later in the same book he identifies eating meat sacrificed to idols as a stumbling block to those with a "weak conscience" (8:1-13). In Romans he remarks that Israel, having been called in the gospel to seek righteousness by faith, "stumbled at that stumbling stone," and then adds this prophetic commentary from Isaiah:

> "Behold, I lay in Zion a stumbling stone and rock of offense,
> And whoever believes on Him will not be put to shame" (Rom. 9:32-33).

Jesus himself, then, is the ultimate stumbling block. His call to forsake sin and self-righteousness, and trust in him alone for salvation instead, is either too demanding or too humbling for many to accept. But there are other stumbling blocks in the way of faith, of a more rationalizing, intellectual sort. As philosophers Kreeft and Tacelli have observed, one of the important tasks in apologetics is "clearing some of the roadblocks and rubble that prevent people from taking the idea of divine revelation seriously."[1]

Accordingly, I have organized the main content of this book to address four intellectual stumbling blocks

Introduction

that seem to frequently stand in the way of Christian faith. I call these the four "E's": *evil, evidence, evolution,* and *exclusivism.*

I decided to begin with evil for two reasons. First, I think evil is a universal problem, in that it affects absolutely everyone at some level. Second, some of the most powerful arguments offered by atheists and naturalists make appeal to the "problem of evil," i.e. the seeming incongruity between the goodness of an omnipotent God on one hand, and the injustice of excruciating suffering of innocents on the other. Next is a discussion of evidence for the faith – specifically the extent of the believer's burden of proof, and a reply to the timeworn accusation that there is "not even a shred of evidence" for the resurrection of Jesus or the existence of the Christian God. A critique of contemporary naturalistic evolutionary theory follows, with analysis of attendant beliefs like the certainty of scientific knowledge and the inherent goodness of technology. Now I admit that trying to refute "evolution" in one chapter, or even one book, would be a bit like trying to eat an elephant in a single sitting. Despite what its leading spokesmen might say, that's not because there is such a huge "mountain of evidence" for evolution, but rather because evolution is an ill-defined, unjustifiably wide-ranging, indeed continually *evolving* theory. Last in the main section is a review and critique of postmodern inclusivism. In that postmodern inclusivism asserts a blanket denial of truth as such – including the truth of Christianity – it clearly amounts to another major stumbling block against faith in Jesus Christ.

Mission-Centered Apologetics

Of course there are other important issues in apologetics, such as purported contradictions in the biblical narratives, but I've found that most of the major objections relate in some way to the four E's. For instance, the argument from "divine hiddenness" can be reframed as basically a new take on the old argument from evil. Arguments to the effect that God is an incoherent or overly abstract concept usually derive from accepting the assertion that there is no positive evidence for a Christian view of God in the first place. Claims that science will eventually solve all the mysteries of the universe and render the supernatural irrelevant, or that technology will eventually solve all the practical problems currently confronting humanity, can typically be traced to, or at minimum associated with, an uncritical acceptance of philosophical naturalism that underlies textbook evolutionary theory. And so on.

Apologetics and Servanthood

All that said, I should stress again that my purpose is centered on mission. The aim here is not to enable apologists to showcase their vast knowledge or their debating skills, or to demonstrate a resolve to continue their arguments *ad infinitum*, never allowing an opponent the last word. To the contrary, apologists and evangelists should be equipped to make arguments strong enough to withstand the disadvantage of their opponents not only having the last word, but the first. More importantly, they should be equipped to dialogue effectively enough that what might begin as an

Introduction

argument often becomes a friendly conversation, and finally a prayer of conversion.

I mentioned First Peter 3:15 earlier as the paradigm "apologist's verse," but honestly I'm not sure it really qualifies. First Peter was specifically written to encourage Christians to maintain their faith and their testimony in the face of persecution and suffering. So when Peter tells us to "always be ready to give a defense to everyone who asks you a reason for the hope that is in you," he is essentially saying that we need to be prepared to explain why anyone should think living for Jesus is really worth the trouble. The context is not abstract philosophical questions in a university classroom, but maintaining a living faith while facing the threat of persecution at the hands of the powerful Roman state. In other words, the early Christians had to have far more than rational arguments, but a testimony of confidence, joy and spiritual strength in a dangerously hostile environment.

For me, Second Timothy 2:23-26 actually best describes the ministry of apologetics in a typical contemporary setting. Paul in these verses depicts the evangelist-apologist as a wise servant who confronts error but avoids contention, all the while keeping a heart for winning his hearers:

> But avoid foolish and ignorant disputes, knowing that they generate strife. And a servant of the Lord must not quarrel but be gentle to all, able to teach, patient, in humility correcting those who are in opposition, if God perhaps will grant them repentance, so that they may know the truth, and that

they may come to their senses and escape the snare of the devil, having been taken captive by him to do his will.

Notice first the call to avoid *foolishness* in disputes, which implies getting caught up in emotional tirades and wasting time in unresolvable conflicts. Additionally Paul instructs us to avoid *ignorance* in disputes, which means either that we avoid disputes altogether – not really possible for people preaching the gospel – or that we grow in knowledge of the issues that typically arise. Again there is an admonition against quarreling (arguing for its own sake), contrasted with an appeal to servanthood, that is, to gentleness, patience and humility in carefully and wisely teaching others the truth. Finally, Paul suggests that once correction has been offered the wise minister will leave the matter in God's hands: "if perhaps God will grant them repentance, so that they may know the truth…" In other words, no attempt should be made to force the issue or rub the noses of nonbelievers in the truth.

The chapters to follow are written in the hope that Christians may be equipped to minister the gospel to skeptical hearers just as Paul describes in the verses above – as servants of the Lord.

2. EVIL AND THE PROBLEM OF SUFFERING

If there is any truth about which philosophers, theologians, journalists and political pundits of all stripes agree, it is that our world is plagued with serious and abundant evils. From the beginnings of recorded history to the present, human experience has been shot through with pain. To a disturbing degree, deep suffering and injustice marks – and for some, seems to even *define* – human existence.

Consider for example the highly publicized case of serial sex abuser Jeffrey Epstein. Here a privileged "financier" amassed a huge fortune by what even close friends and associates say are mysterious means; used that wealth to lure young girls from poor neighborhoods – with promises of a lucrative career – onto his private jet and an island where he sexually abused them; when first exposed for his crimes received a "shockingly light sentence" through the influence of some powerful and corrupt friends; was able as a result to continue abusing young girls at will; and when finally charged and convicted in a serious way (facing forty-five years in prison for sex trafficking), was either murdered or committed suicide. The whole lurid tale is an object lesson in evil, injustice, and the suffering of poor and vulnerable people.[2]

As horrific as Epstein's case is, it represents just the tip of the iceberg. A modern-day version of slavery, sex trafficking has become an immensely profitable industry, raking in roughly $100 billion a year.[3] Notoriously, sex traffickers deliberately target the most vulnerable girls they can find: the poor and the homeless, foster children, and victims of neglect and abuse. The average age of these girls upon starting their "new life"? Thirteen. Once captured, they are essentially raped, repeatedly, up to fifteen times a day, and when failing to "perform" their acts to the satisfaction of clients, beaten or even killed. Statistics reveal further that their clientele are not lonely, desperate or insecure men, but wealthy, married professionals with plenty of disposable income to burn. It's all enough to make one enraged, if not nauseated.

Of course, sex trafficking is but one of countless expressions of evil in the world. Besides the assaults of criminals and abuses of tyrants upon the vulnerable and unsuspecting, there are the corrupt leaders, judges and bureaucrats that enable such acts to continue. Beyond all that still, the natural world unleashes death and destruction upon humanity in the way of hurricanes, tornadoes, famines, earthquakes, mudslides, tsunamis, and countless sicknesses and diseases. These all strike indiscriminately at both rich and poor, religious and unbelieving, morally responsible and selfishly unscrupulous.

Last November an old friend of ours, a bold but kindhearted, decades-long faithful believer in Christ, passed away. She had been stricken with a form of cancer that left her with only one arm and loss of function in her only hand. I remember hearing of her painful plight and asking myself, "Why her?" The patriarch Job was well-known, even by God himself, for his righteousness, yet he endured such excruciating pain and devastating loss that he made heartfelt declarations like, "My eye will never again see good." Even now Christians in places like Syria and Nigeria are suffering the worst imaginable kinds of persecution, being driven from their homes, tortured, and killed.

All these facts and incidents serve to call further attention to the obvious: that life often seems deeply unfair, unjust, and unbearably painful. In the throes of suffering, what philosophers have called the "problem of evil" is not only a serious intellectual problem but becomes a deeply emotional *personal* problem.

Evil in the Church

One especially relevant form of evil that bears mentioning in the context of Christian apologetics is the problem of mistreatment and hypocrisy within the church. Examples unfortunately abound throughout the churches, and throughout church history. Though a standout believer and defender of the faith himself, Dietrich Bonhoeffer nonetheless had to confess:

> It is just not true that every word of criticism directed against contemporary preaching is a deliberate rejection of Christ and proceeds from the spirit of Antichrist. So many people come to church with a genuine desire to hear what we have to say, yet they are always going back home with the uncomfortable feeling that we are making it too difficult for them to come to Jesus… They are convinced that it is not the Word of Jesus himself

> that puts them off, but the superstructure of human, institutional, and doctrinal elements in our preaching. Of course we know all the answers to these objections, and those answers certainly make it easy for us to slide out of our responsibilities. But perhaps it would be just as well to ask ourselves whether we do not in fact often act as obstacles to Jesus and his Word.[4]

In other words, it's possible that as Christians *we ourselves* can be stumbling blocks to the very message we preach. It would probably discourage most believers to realize just how many atheists today have lost their faith not because of evil generally, but because of evil in the particularly exasperating form of glaring hypocrisy and abuse of trust among religious people professing the name of Jesus, including high-profile church leaders. If there has ever been a good reason for Christians to take stock of what we're doing and reexamine how we conduct ourselves in the church, this is it.

A related issue is the problem of false teaching (or in some cases a lack of teaching altogether) concerning pain and suffering. Perhaps nothing is more discouraging for me during times of deep distress than bearing the reproach, not of the secular, unbelieving world, but of fellow Christians and Christian leaders who teach that suffering is a sure sign of disobedience or unbelief. For example, popular "prosperity" preachers like Kenneth Copeland and Creflo Dollar, even while preaching to desperately poor and afflicted listeners, openly declare that poverty and sickness are the direct results of personal sin or selfishness.

Evil and the Problem of Suffering

So it is that in certain contemporary Christian circles Paul's famous exhortation to love in 1 Corinthians 13 might be rephrased, "And now abide power, status, and wealth; but the greatest of these is wealth." Now if it's true that wealth is a function of faith, then it seems the richest men would have to have the greatest faith. Yet three of the richest men in the world – Warren Buffett, Larry Ellison and Charles Koch – are atheists. Clearly something is wrong with the simple correlation of faith with material prosperity.

One reason poor and suffering people tend to keep their distance from the church, then, is that so often the church openly looks down upon them and shames them. The apostles in the New Testament, particularly James, explicitly forbade the church from taking this attitude. To the contrary, the apostles declared that there is *no* shame, but rather glory and honor, in suffering in and for the faith. "If anyone suffers as a Christian," said Peter for example, "let him not be ashamed, but let him glorify God..." (1 Pet. 4:16).

Entire books in the New Testament appear written for the express purpose of encouraging saints in the throes of hardship, among them Second Timothy, Hebrews, James, First Peter and Revelation. Jesus obviously suffered greatly, and warned that his disciples, not being greater than their Master, would suffer likewise. Paul often listed out his many sufferings and tribulations as proof of his apostleship. Yet many Christian leaders today maintain not merely that God's will for all of us is continual blessings, but that any *lack* of blessings is evidence of a "spirit of poverty," or disobedience, or some other spiritual failing.[5]

This was the fallacy of Job's friends: that the only possible explanation for Job's great sufferings was his own sin. One of their many unfounded accusations against Job was that he must have abused and defrauded the innocent. Of course such an argument is a nonstarter; for on the premise that a person's suffering directly correlates with that same person's sin, it would be impossible for Job to treat others any worse than they already deserve. This "theology of retribution," as it's sometimes called, would lead us to believe abject moral and spiritual nonsense – that small children in Africa, for example, are slowly starving to death because they have failed to repent of their sins. The whole notion is transparently, shamefully false.

The Problem of Evil

When people facing pain, tragedy and injustice begin to think about God, the question almost always arises: *Why?* Why does life have to be so cruel? Why doesn't God do anything to fix the terrible situation? Why does God allow it in the first place? Why does this have to happen to me, and yet nothing like this ever seems to happen to brazenly arrogant, selfish or dishonest people? To the extent that they prevent us from believing in God's goodness, or even God's existence, acts and occurrences of evil are *stumbling blocks* to faith.

So what exactly *is* this "problem of evil"? Though formulations of the problem of evil are as old as the ancient Greek philosopher Epicurus, they have become more sophisticated and varied in recent years. Philosophers these days distinguish the *logical* problem of evil

Evil and the Problem of Suffering

from the *evidential* problem of evil, for example, and further distinguish *moral* evil from *natural* evil. Nonetheless, the core problem can generally be boiled down to the following set of propositions:

1. God is all-powerful.
2. God is all-good.
3. Evil exists.

It seems one may pick any two, but not all three. As Epicurus is said to have put it, "Is God willing to prevent evil, but not able? Then he is not omnipotent. Is he able, but not willing? Then he is malevolent. Is he both able and willing? Then whence cometh evil? Is he neither able nor willing? Then why call him God?"[6] Given that the existence of evil is not reconcilable with the existence of a God who is both all-good and all-powerful, the problem of evil presents a serious challenge to the Christian faith, because evil clearly exists. Just as clearly, the people we seek to win to Christ have experienced evil themselves. For this reason Christian evangelists should, above all else, demonstrate compassion for those enduring suffering and expressing the emotions that so often come with it.

To address the problem *intellectually*, on the other hand, we should probably first examine the logic of it. Now if the set of propositions in question is not in fact contradictory, then it may be possible for all three propositions to be true at the same time. As it happens, and as philosopher Alvin Plantinga has pointed out, the set is not in fact contradictory.[7] Indeed, no single one of these propositions contradicts either of the other two, let alone both. For there to be a contradiction, there would have to be a negation, either stated or implied, of at least one of the propositions within the set, such as: *God is not all-powerful*; *God is not all-good*; or *Evil does not exist*. Plantinga went on to demonstrate that as long as it's merely *possible* that temporary evil is necessary for God to create a "greater good," the logical argument from evil fails. At most, then, the relationship between God and evil is intuitively problematic rather than formally contradictory.

Another answer can be traced back to the great fourth century bishop Aurelius Augustine, who argued in the *Confessions* that the existence of evil actually entails the existence of God, in that one cannot recognize evil except as a corruption or "privation" of an original good. "I understood therefore that thou madest all things good."[8] Moral goodness and virtue are positive characteristics; evil is a denial or repudiation of them. Following Augustine's lead, I have argued along similar lines: "Thus a hateful, cruel and lazy man is also loveless, merciless and shiftless, whereas it would make no sense to say that a loving, merciful and diligent man is hate-less, cruelty-less and laziness-less."[9] On this reading, evil is not so much a "thing" in itself but a description of life apart from the presence and grace of God.

Moreover, if evil cannot be explained in light of God's existence, we are still in need of an explanation for it, which most non-Christian views seem unable to provide. Hinduism, for instance, regards evil as essentially an illusion (*maya*) derived from ignorance of the only reality, the Brahman. According to modern scientific naturalism, what we call "evil" is little more than an epiphenomenon of biological evolution. In that case "evil" is a perfectly natural state of affairs obtaining within a perfectly natural (amoral) universe. It's not likely, then, given the truth of evolutionary naturalism, that we would even *recognize* evil as such. The fact that we *do* recognize it as such therefore makes evil a problem for both Hinduism and naturalism. Christianity, on the other hand, not only permits but *predicts* the ongoing presence of evil in the world as a reality resulting from human transgression of God's holy commandments.

While the above basic Christian responses to evil ring true with me personally, many skeptics are looking for something more like a *theodicy*, a complete and rational "justification" of God's goodness and power given the reality of evil in the world. In other words, for many people it's not enough to know that it's merely *possible* that God exists alongside the experiences we call evil, or to know that other belief systems may not explain evil all that well. They want to know that Christianity explains it sufficiently, and regardless of other belief systems. That's understandable, and we will examine theodicies momentarily. But we should pause and take note: it may be that evil doesn't make sense simply because it's not *supposed* to make sense. At bottom evil is moral irrationality, after all, and not something any of us should be expected to properly understand or manage. That would be precisely why God warns us to steer clear of it.

Popular Theodicies

It should be admitted up front that full-blown, well-developed theodicies are hard to come by, a fact which perhaps helps explain why arguments from evil remain the most common justification for atheism. Here I think Christians should still encourage skeptics to consider two of the most successful theodicies on record: the "free will theodicy," associated with Plantinga's free will defense, and the "soul-making theodicy" developed by John Hick. I also have sketched out a third, which I have called the "theodicy of incompleteness" and which I will review briefly.

What is now known as the free will theodicy has its historical roots in the comprehensive theology of Augustine, but today is largely attributable to the work of Alvin Plantinga. Through publication of his now-famous "free will defense," Plantinga has managed to prove, to the satisfaction of a majority of philosophers and theologians, that the logical argument from evil does not go through. In other words, atheists who contend, often with seemingly sophisticated arguments, that the problem of evil logically disproves the existence of God have not in fact successfully made their case. But it's one thing to show that a critic has not proven the Christian position false; it's quite another to show that our position is true, or even plausible.

A free will *theodicy* therefore has more ground to cover than a mere free will *defense*. Nonetheless, the concept of human free will to choose between live options (sometimes called *libertarian* free will), does seem to supply a coherent explanation for evil and the consequent suffering that plagues our lives here on earth, at least when combined with the biblical data. For example, the New Testament declares that Adam's sin unleashed a curse upon the earth, and that *the whole creation* now "groans and toils" under the weight of that curse (Rom. 8:22) – which makes for a sound biblical-theological explanation for natural disasters and other forms of evil or suffering normally considered natural rather than moral evil. In other words, according to Scripture natural evil derives directly from the original moral evil committed in the Garden.

One major problem confronts any free will theodicy, however, and that is the problem of…well, *free will*. What I mean specifically is the problem of free will in the afterlife. The difficulty is this: if free will is essential to meaningful human flourishing, and if free will entails the ever-present possibility of committing sins that cause suffering, then we are evidently left with two logical alternatives: (1) there can be no free will in heaven; or (2) there may be suffering in heaven. Neither of these propositions seems satisfactory given what it means to be eternally joyful in an eternal paradise, and for that reason the free will theodicy falls short of a complete explanation for evil within a Christian framework.

Anticipated in its basic form by Irenaeus in the second century, John Hick's soul-making theodicy unfortunately holds up no better, and arguably much worse, than the free will theodicy. As Hick sees it, humans have been deliberately created (I say "created" loosely, given Hick's flat denial of Genesis as historical narrative) by God in a default condition of hardship and spiritual immaturity. In making his presence and goodness difficult to detect in a world shot through with suffering, God creates "epistemic distance" between himself and his creatures, so that we might freely learn right and wrong, and come to faith in God in a more meaningful way than by his simply revealing himself to us. We essentially *learn* to trust in and embrace his goodness, which makes for a deeper and richer commitment.

The main strength of the soul-making theodicy is that it not only accounts for natural evil, but actually makes natural evil a necessary element of a meaningful life of faith. The main weakness of the soul-making theodicy is that so much suffering apparently cannot be worked into a rationally defensible soul-making purpose. On Hick's view, even the most gratuitous, unjust suffering of innocents at the hands of capricious tormenters somehow builds character and encourages faith. But of course this often is simply not the case. Some suffering is so intense and unjust that it completely overwhelms, and even destroys completely, the sufferer. A person being slowly tortured to death by a sadistic serial killer presumably does not learn much of God's grace and goodness in the process (much less does the killer). Moreover, the very notion of "epistemic distance," as Michael Martin has pointed out, would seem to justify atheism at least as easily as it would faith in God. "Epistemic distance...creates a situation where any attempt to come to God would be *initially* epistemologically unjustified....Yet this irrational act is the one that makes entrance into heaven possible..."[10]

Evil and the Problem of Suffering

Given these criticisms, it seems that the best theodicy would combine the strengths of both the free will and soul-making versions. Whereas a free will theodicy (at least a biblical version of it) *predicts* natural evil as the unintended consequence of human willful spiritual disobedience, a soul-making theodicy actually *utilizes* natural evil for the stated purpose of moral development and growth in faith. Even then, there are limitations to how much suffering we can explain or justify, and Christians need to acknowledge this in the interests of truth and compassion. "It must be admitted," say philosophers Evans and Manis, "that, as full-fledged theodicies, neither free will arguments alone nor such arguments taken in conjunction with a soul-making argument can be established conclusively."[11] But is this really surprising? If scientists can acknowledge their inability to explain certain aspects of the physical universe, Christians can acknowledge their inability to explain certain aspects of human existence within that same universe.

Other Theodicies

That brings me to my own modest contribution to the literature on theodicy, what I have called a "theodicy of incompleteness." Having read a bit about Kurt Gödel's incompleteness theorems, I realized a few years ago that our present experience in this universe could be likened to a mathematical system, in which there is a true statement whose truth nonetheless cannot be ascertained only from the axioms known to be true within that system. To explain I borrowed an analogy from Rudy Rucker, of a "universal truth machine" (one that outputs only true statements) whose operator inputs the following statement: "The truth machine will never say that this sentence is true." Then the operator asks the truth machine if the statement is true or false:

> If the truth machine decides the sentence is true, it cannot say so (because the sentence states that the truth machine will not say it is true). If the truth machine decides the sentence is false, then again it cannot say so (because it only answers with true statements) – yet its failure to say so is precisely what the sentence says of the truth machine. It is true, then, that the truth machine will never say that the sentence is true. Though true in itself, the undecidability of the sentence *for the truth machine* means that its truth cannot be recognized by that same machine.[12]

I then suggested that the truth of a particular theological statement – namely: "God's act of creating beings free to choose between good and evil is morally justifiable" – appears equally, though less formally, undecidable. If true, it seems to follow that the freedom to choose evil is morally justifiable. If false, it seems to follow that freedom to choose good is *not* morally justifiable. Given our understandings of *freedom, good, evil*, and their implications, neither answer is fully satisfactory.

If we understand the eternal kingdom of heaven as a system that *transcends* the present system of this world, however, it may well be that the coexistence of

Evil and the Problem of Suffering

God and evil is true in a way that is currently inaccessible owing simply to the limitations of living within the present system: "Although the logical compatibility of evil and divine benevolence, of free will and eternal blessedness, cannot be strictly proven within the system of this world, Scripture posits its provability in the larger transcendent system of the kingdom."[13]

Before concluding discussion of Christian theodicies, we should take a brief look at one notably peculiar form of theodicy, hardly a theodicy at all – namely, the *theodicy of protest*. I mention theodicy of protest because it speaks the kind of indignant, defiant language common to nonbelievers, but from the perspective of a believer. John K. Roth for example asks pointedly, "If God is all-powerful, why could he not prevent the Holocaust? Why could he not prevent the most horrific evils?" These are the sorts of questions even the most theologically orthodox of believers have often thought, but rarely out loud. To those who would appeal to God's saving acts in history, like the Exodus or the resurrection of Jesus, Roth argues that these events go against the flow of "history's ongoing testimony." He concludes, "God's saving acts in the world are too few and far between."[14]

Protest theodicies not only resonate with hurting people, but have clear biblical precedent in the trials and moral objections of Job, and therefore merit at least a place in the discussion. For my part, I believe "protestors" like Roth to be passionate, courageous, and well-intended – as Job was – but also ultimately wrong in their judgments about God's abilities and intentions – as Job was.

Evil and the Gospel

What's most important for mission-minded Christians, and for those who hear our message, is to note how the problem of evil relates to the gospel we preach. Again, my operating assumption here is that arguments from evil are at least as much emotionally as intellectually driven. The problem ultimately is not a technical logical incongruity between the concept of God and the concept of evil, but a subjective disconnect between our expectations of what God's goodness should mean for us and what we actually experience in life. We simply expect *better treatment* in a world created by a good and powerful God.

During my own experiences of suffering terrifying depressions, or lying betrayals, or unjust financial setbacks, I have never much doubted God's omnipotence, let alone his existence. What I *have* doubted is his goodness. I dare say the same is probably true of most professing atheists. Having interacted with many atheists over many years, I would suggest that most cases of "atheism" can be explained in terms of *cognitive dissonance* theory, in which disappointed and frustrated believers find themselves having to somehow reconcile their growing belief that God is cruel, capricious, indifferent, etc., with their existing belief that God is good. When the conviction that God is all-powerful is thrown into the mix, this cognitive dissonance gives way to a powerful *emotional* dissonance. Then the problem is not so much that Christian faith is illogical, but simply too terrifying to seriously contemplate.

Evil and the Problem of Suffering

To minister the gospel in the face of overpowering evil and unbelief, we first need to know just what the gospel is. Most New Testament scholars would concur that the gospel, as Jesus preached it, is all about the kingdom of God. In Matthew and Mark, the good news is that "the kingdom of heaven is at hand" (Mk. 1:15; Mt. 4:17), and elsewhere in Matthew Jesus says that "this gospel of the kingdom will be preached in all the world…" (24:14). In John, Jesus says that the kingdom of God cannot be seen unless one is "born again," and therefore his kingdom is "not of this world" (Joh. 3:3; 18:36). Through the blood of Christ, eternal life in the kingdom of God has been made accessible to all men. In Luke, however, Jesus unpacks the meaning of the gospel in more individually therapeutic terms, citing the prophet Isaiah:

> "The Spirit of the Lord is upon Me,
> Because He has anointed Me
> To preach the gospel to the poor;
> He has sent Me to heal the brokenhearted,
> To proclaim liberty to the captives
> And recovery of sight to the blind,
> To set at liberty those who are oppressed;
> To proclaim the acceptable year of the Lord"
> (Lk. 4:18-19).

Here Jesus describes the recipients of the gospel – the poor, the brokenhearted, the captives, the blind, the oppressed – and promises them healing, liberty, restoration, and acceptance. These are the residents of the kingdom of God, as Jesus describes them again in the

Mission-Centered Apologetics

Beatitudes (Mt. 5:3-12; Lk. 6:20-23). Thus it may be said that in the gospel, Jesus has come to personally confront and overcome evil – not by simply *eradicating* it but by ministering healing and grace to those most affected by it. Implicit in his mission is the acknowledgment that evil is a serious, deadly reality, but a reality he is personally authorized and empowered to overcome. At the heart of the gospel of the kingdom is the promise of the victory of Jesus in his confrontation with the powers of darkness on our behalf. "The coming of the kingdom of God involves God's intervention in the course of human history. His power breaks into the affairs of men, confronting the forces that withstand him and imprison people, and interrupting the course of society."[15]

Keeping in mind that for most people the problem of evil is more emotional than logical, Christians laboring in the harvest field would be wise to follow Jesus' lead and minister to hurting people with a similar spirit of compassion. While it may well be that some of our hearers are in pain precisely because of their own sin, and while the gospel certainly calls them to repentance, the fact is that if there is no compassion in the message, it almost certainly will not be received. That's not necessarily because the hearers are sinful and rebellious, but because for them a message of judgment will only cause more pain and reinforce their already deep feelings of brokenness and rejection; and in that case they may be sadly unable to hear the *good* in the good news at all. People undergoing deep suffering do not need correction and instruction nearly as

Evil and the Problem of Suffering

much as they need assurance of grace – exactly what the gospel provides.

Beyond the compassion of the gospel toward suffering people in the present, moreover, is the hope of the gospel for the future. The kingdom of God has powerfully invaded the present through Jesus Christ, it's true, but not yet in its fullness. It seems that for every statement of Jesus suggesting that the kingdom of God is "within you" or has "come upon you," there are two more making it clear that the kingdom is still coming – that no one knows the day or hour, that we need to watch and prepare for "that day," lest we be caught unawares. For this reason biblical scholars often maintain that the kingdom is both "already and not yet." Faithful ministers of the gospel, therefore, preach not only healing and compassion in the face of present evil, but the full and final victory over evil at the end of time. The future abolition of all sin and suffering in Christ's everlasting kingdom is the ultimate solution to the problem of evil.

3. EVIDENCE AND THE BURDEN OF PROOF

The issue of *evidence* for the gospel has become more important in recent years, as *empiricism*, an outgrowth of both eighteenth-century Enlightenment philosophy and twenty-first century devotion to science, has come to be regarded as the only philosophical outlook capable of ensuring the acquisition of knowledge. Accordingly, today's skeptics and critics often make statements like, "No truth claim is worth consideration unless it is supported by evidence" – apparently not noticing any paradoxes or contradictions in such statements. This prevalent outlook is bolstered not so much by anything self-evident, let alone scientifically testable, about empiricism itself, but by the continuing popular advancement of the scientific enterprise.

As science and the scientific method offer explanations for an increasingly broad range of phenomena – in fields as diverse as physics and forensics – the presumed role of scientific evidence in discovering truth grows accordingly. So strong has this basic philosophical prejudice become in the mind of the public that words like "belief," "faith," and "conviction," once associated with moral ideals and wholeness of character, are now taken as indicators of ignorance or intellectual cowardice. In other words, supplying *evidence* for a proposition or theological position is now something like a moral imperative. This rather odd modern corollary to traditional morality appears traceable to the evidentialism of William Clifford, who argued famously that "it is wrong, always, everywhere, and for anyone, to believe anything upon insufficient evidence."[16] Thus one possible consequence of the increasing popularity of evidentialism would be a certain sense of shame or embarrassment heaped upon Christians (or potential Christians), who might be under the impression that there really is "no evidence" to support the Christian faith. Who wants to be likened to a small child refusing to give up his belief in Santa Claus or the Tooth Fairy? In this case old-fashioned peer pressure could well play a part in keeping prospective believers from openly acknowledging belief as such. Given the basic New Testament dictum that salvation is "by faith," this kind of socially enforced aversion to belief could mean for many the difference between spiritual life and death.

It turns out that the presumed dichotomy between truth and knowledge, on one hand, and belief and faith, on the other, is simply a *false* dichotomy. Here we should recall the philosopher's basic definition of knowledge itself, as "justified true belief." Or as Plato put it, "Knowledge is true opinion." Indeed, most of what passes for knowledge could not possibly be had *apart* from implicitly accepting certain foundational beliefs – what philosophers have called "properly basic beliefs." One cannot discover a truth of science using the "scientific method," for example, without accepting as true various assumptions inherent in the scientific method itself (the existence of physical objects independent of our perceptions, or the axioms of logic

Evidence and the Burden of Proof

and mathematics) – even if those assumptions aren't themselves scientifically testable. The important point to note here is not that belief always entails knowledge, but that knowledge always entails belief. A moment's reflection suggests this to be the case; for how can one possibly *know* something to be true without *believing* it to be true at the same time?

Evidence and the Absence of Evidence

Next to the argument from evil, the most common argument raised against the Christian faith appears to be simply this: *there is no evidence for it*. Mischievous skeptics often frame this assertion as a diligent search for truth: "I want to believe in God and be a Christian, but I have found no evidence that God exists or that Christianity is true. Can someone provide me with at least a tiny shred of evidence?" Reacting to this sort of provocation, Christians sometimes fall into traps like arguing back that there is no evidence that God does *not* exist or that Christianity is *not* true. While that response is technically correct, it's also a fallacy. In most cases, trying to prove a negative is a fool's errand. One may be able to prove, in principle, that a Bigfoot exists, by trapping him and showing him to the public; but no amount of searching yet failing to find a Bigfoot will ever prove that no Bigfoot exists. He may be lurking just over the next hill, after all.

So, while a Christian would be wrong to ask an atheist for evidence of God's nonexistence, the flip side of the above observation is that, with few exceptions, *absence of evidence is not evidence of absence*.

Precisely because Bigfoot may be lurking over the next hill, to positively affirm that Bigfoot does not exist assumes more than can be rationally warranted. Atheists, then, would be wrong to pronounce atheism proven even if it were the case that no evidence whatever could be found for God's existence.[17]

With these sorts of considerations in mind, most atheists contend that the responsibility of providing evidence lies strictly with the believer (the one making a positive claim), not the skeptic. Ever since the late great philosopher Antony Flew published his famous essay "The Presumption of Atheism,"[18] it has become a sort of unspoken rule of Christian-atheist debates that the Christian bears the sole burden of proof. In advocating this presumption of atheism, Flew compared the Christians' burden to prove their case to the prosecution's burden to prove theirs in a court of law. Thus until the Christian proves the existence of God beyond a reasonable doubt, atheism is "presumed innocent" of being in error.

Now on the definition of *atheism* as a mere "lack of belief," this seems reasonable enough: the burden of proof, as Flew said, lies "on the proposition, not the opposition." If I were to swear to my wife that I just had a conversation with a leprechaun, it would be reasonable for her to challenge me to prove my claim, and it would be *un*reasonable for me to challenge her to *dis*prove my claim in response – because the claim cannot be disproven even in principle. Flew himself was careful to point out that what he proposes is a procedural rather than substantive principle, so that when properly applied in a debate, the presumption of

Evidence and the Burden of Proof

atheism presupposes nothing about the strength or weakness of the Christian position.

To my knowledge, however, Flew never mentioned what should happen to the burden of proof once a Christian undertakes to not only accept that burden but to satisfy it (or claim to satisfy it) by providing various forms of evidence. It seems to me that once relevant facts are brought in for examination, the burden of proof shifts. A skeptic at that point can no longer claim to simply lack belief because there is "no evidence." To rationally maintain lack of belief (or continue to assert the irrationality of belief), good arguments have to be made against the evidence that has already been provided.

As mentioned earlier, some truths are properly basic – that is, ascertained or demonstrated prior to, or apart from, any consideration of evidence. The truth that I exist, for example, is for me entirely self-evident. Other truths are the product of logical deduction, or mathematical calculation, or simple observation. There is no "evidence" available, for instance, to confirm that the conclusion of a sound logical inference is really true; it just follows from basic logical entailments we all intuitively recognize to be valid. Nor is there "evidence" that my perceptions of physical objects in the room around me correspond with real objects that exist independently of my perceptions. The content of those perceptions, given that we trust them, may be evidence for *other* truths, but clearly they cannot be *evidence* that the perceptions themselves correspond to reality. One answer to the evidential objection, then, is that not all rationally warranted truths are inductively derived.

Mission-Centered Apologetics

And if not all rationally warranted truths are inductively derived, then the existence of God and various truths of Christian doctrine may be self-evidently true even if there were no external evidence for them. This suggests that it may be possible to know that God exists by no other means than the faith that God himself has given to us.[19] In that case it may be possible for the Christian to rationally maintain faith without taking on the implied burden of proof in the way of evidence.

Evidence for Christianity

Nonetheless, most skeptics leaning toward a scientific epistemology require some form of evidence as a prerequisite to knowledge. And Christian evangelists-apologists doing our work in a spirit of servanthood should be willing to accommodate them, which suggests that we still need to both *define* and *supply* evidence. Evidence has to do with inductive rather than deductive inference, and therefore is usually defined in terms of probability rather than binary true/false determinations. According to Richard Swinburne, *evidence* for a hypothesis can be defined as any new information that increases its probability, i.e. that makes its probability higher than it would have been otherwise. For example, because finding Tom's fingerprints at the scene of the crime renders the hypothesis that he was involved more likely, Tom's fingerprints at the scene of the crime constitutes *evidence* for the hypothesis that he was involved.

As Swinburne explains further, the intrinsic or "prior" probabilities of the evidence and the hypothesis

Evidence and the Burden of Proof

can usually be plugged into a Bayesian framework (incorporating Bayes' theorem) to more precisely calculate the degree to which the evidence succeeds in confirming the hypothesis.[20]

When challenged by atheists to provide evidence for Christianity, I usually will supply a list much like the following:

1. Cosmological evidence suggesting an absolute beginning (of both space and time) of the universe.

2. The apparent fine-tuning of life-permitting physical constants regulating the universe.

3. Numerous instances of specified complexity (or "functional complexity" or "irreducible complexity") in nature.

4. General human awareness of transcendent or "objective" moral rules.

5. The historical origin, worldwide dispersion and persecution, and subsequent physical restoration of the nation of Israel, in keeping with the prophetic message of the Old Testament

6. The equally prophetic, miraculous ministry of Jesus Christ, historically preserved in thousands of early manuscripts derived from originals dated to within a generation of his resurrection and corroborated by the writings of early church fathers.

Mission-Centered Apologetics

7. The birth of the early church, in Jerusalem, on the preaching of the resurrection, and in the face of violent persecution.

8. The remarkably sudden, complete conversion of Saul of Tarsus, formerly a leader in the earliest efforts to destroy the Christian movement.

9. Independent corroboration of countless details of the New Testament narrative in extrabiblical documentary and archaeological evidence.

Taking on the full responsibility of an apologist, I have to not only lay out the evidence to my atheist friends, but stand ready to explain how each fact in evidence supports the truth of the Christian faith. To take the first example: cosmological evidence suggesting an absolute beginning of the universe is also evidence for the creation of the heavens and the earth described in Genesis, because without that evidence we could look out at the universe and just as easily believe it had existed in its present state forever; thus the evidence for an absolute beginning makes the absolute beginning described in Genesis much more probable than it would have been otherwise.

From the particular perspective of Christian theism – as opposed to a "generic" theism unassociated with any particular peoples or traditions – the most important of the facts listed above would be items 5-9; and given that the resurrection is the ultimate vindication of Christianity, seven may be the most critical of all. If a certain hypothesis (in this case the resurrection)

Evidence and the Burden of Proof

is well supported, or predicted, by the evidence, and the evidence for it would not be expected otherwise, that hypothesis enjoys great explanatory power. So it is that the facts surrounding the death of Jesus and subsequent disappearance of his body powerfully attest to the truth of the resurrection. In addition to the highly unlikely birth of the church in Jerusalem on the preaching of the resurrection are other important facts bearing on the case: the empty tomb and the reported post-resurrection appearances of Jesus to the disciples. Those facts are all improbable in themselves, yet the resurrection all but completely explains those same facts, making it a powerful explanation.

I say "all but completely" because there is a certain technical objection to the suggestion that the resurrection has great explanatory power. As Jeffery Jay Lowder at the *Secular Outpost* pointed out to me a few years ago, it may be true that Jesus "moved the stone, walked out of the tomb, and appeared to different people. But the content of R [the resurrection] doesn't include those activities. All R says is that Jesus rose from the dead." Thus it may be that Jesus reanimated but never left the tomb, that he carefully slipped out of the tomb undetected and moved to Tibet where he lives to this day, etc. Therefore, he says, "R [the resurrection] does not *entail* the data. In other words, the probability of Jesus' crucifixion, burial, empty tomb, and postmortem appearances, *conditional upon the assumption that R is true*, is less than 1."[21]

Lowder is correct here, again technically. But while it's true that the resurrection is not a complete explanation, not entailing all the data, it's at least a very strong partial explanation. To arrive at a complete explanation would require adding a few widely attested postulates from the Gospels: (1) Jesus is who he claimed to be: the Son of God, with access to the miracle power of the Father; (2) Jesus predicted that he would rise from the dead after his crucifixion; and (3) Jesus promised to re-commune with his disciples after he had risen from the dead. Those additional postulates, if true, would explain the resurrection; and the resurrection, along with those postulates, would explain the empty tomb and the postmortem appearances, and by extension, the birth of the church in Jerusalem and even the conversion of Saul of Tarsus. In other words, yes – all told, the resurrection "hypothesis" enjoys tremendous explanatory power.

Faced with the abundance of evidence for Christianity, nonbelievers implicitly assume a burden of proof of their own; they have to explain why the evidence cited fails to support the truth of Christianity. Or they can simply bite the bullet and re-assert that there is no evidence for Christianity. (Better still, they can admit that the evidence is sufficient to overcome their doubts and surrender their lives to Jesus Christ in faith!) From what I've experienced as an apologist, the only justification given for asserting that none of the many sources of *proposed* evidence is *actual* evidence, is the fact that none of those sources in itself proves Christianity true. While that objection can scarcely be denied, it ignores two important observations about evidence: (1) Evidence is not truth functional in the way a conclusion in a logically deductive argument might be; for example, no matter how much or how strong

Evidence and the Burden of Proof

the evidence for it, the moon landing *could possibly* have been an incredibly elaborate hoax nonetheless. Therefore evidence will always be compatible with a huge number of hypotheses, not just one – though the hypotheses themselves may vary in terms of simplicity, explanatory scope and explanatory power. (2) Evidence for a hypothesis is thought to be stronger when there is more of it, and more kinds of it, rather than less; so while the "divide and conquer" method of diluting the evidence may be rhetorically effective, it appears that those employing it either do not understand the very nature of evidence-based reasoning or are not acting (or arguing) in good faith. Nonbelievers should not be asking for evidence, if what they really want is not in fact evidence, but instead some kind of ultimately undeniable "proof."

Together the above facts make for a powerful *cumulative case* for the Christian faith. The cumulative case approach to apologetics should appeal to empiricists and evidentialists, in that it takes into account as much evidence as possible and uses it to derive a "best explanation" or "common sense" conclusion, rather than a strictly logical conclusion to a formal argument. In this, apologetics closely parallels arguments for scientific theories known to have considerable explanatory power and scope. Powerful cumulative case arguments have been made to support the resurrection of Christ; and with the set of facts outlined above, I would suggest there is also a strong cumulative case available for the larger truth of Christian theism and the larger body of doctrine we call "the Christian faith."

Evidence and the Gospel

There are basically two options available for Christian evangelists and apologists confronted with the question of evidence. First is the "negative critique" – to point out the inconsistency in asserting that all claims to truth must be justified by the criterion of evidence, when there appears to be no evidence for the assertion itself. Second is the "positive case" – to direct those same skeptics to the evidence for Christian truth. Both tactics have proven useful, and indeed can be used in tandem. In the work of laying out evidence for a genuinely skeptical seeker, as in all evangelistic efforts, we should bear in mind that truth and compassion are vitally and equally important. There are times when honest people struggle with serious doubts. Apologists do their best work, I believe, when ministering graciously to these sorts of tenderhearted skeptics.

Ministers of the gospel should remind hearers that even the most secure, scientifically sound forms of knowledge, according to philosophers, cannot be had without *belief* in something – whether belief in the validity of logic, belief in the reliability of sense experience, or in this case, belief in God. To put it another way: evidence can only do so much. In the light of the fact that all knowledge begins with these sorts of "properly basic beliefs," there is nothing intellectually shameful about faith in God, especially since most people in the world do embrace religious belief of one kind or another. As the New Testament has it in the book of Hebrews, "Now faith is the substance of things hoped for, the evidence of things not seen" (11:1). It could be argued that faith "fills the gap" between evidence and certain conviction.

The life of Jesus himself provides an excellent case study in how to present evidence to skeptical seekers. His dealing with Thomas, in particular, calls attention to the legitimate need for evidence (or at least an *assurance* of evidence), and at the same time, the importance of faith over unbelief. To his sometimes-doubtful disciples, Jesus said in John 14:11, "Believe Me that I am in the Father and the Father in Me, or else believe Me for the sake of the works themselves." Again the idea is that believing in Christ on the basis of his own self-authenticating authority is best; but understanding that the human heart sometimes fails of spiritual courage or conviction, Jesus appeals to the evidence – "the works themselves." The disciples had seen Jesus make remarkable claims and then back them up with remarkable miracles of healing and exorcism. He reminds them of those objective facts to prop up their faltering faith and encourage renewed dedication to God. He proceeds then to challenge them to a life of discipleship, to do the same works in their own lives (John 14:12-14). In so doing he models the spiritual priorities of effective apologetics.

4. EVOLUTION, SCIENCE AND TECHNOLOGY

When I first came to the faith way back in 1985, I honestly had never thought much about the theory of biological evolution. The whole concept of evolution seemed kind of hazy and mysterious, far removed from my experience of Christianity and my firm belief that God was the all-powerful Creator of the world and life within it. That all changed when I began a course entitled "Evolution, Ecology and the Environment" at the University of Texas the next Spring semester. Suddenly I was faced with a sophisticated, detailed and yet thoroughly naturalistic view of the biological world that seemed to leave no room for God's creative activity at all.

While my professor assured me that there was no contradiction between evolution and religious accounts of creation like in the book of Genesis, I could personally see no possibility of reconciliation – and still cannot see it to this day. With due respect to certain of my Christian brothers and sisters who claim to believe the truth of both contemporary evolutionary theory and the narrative of Genesis, I don't think they understand just what evolution, as currently taught in textbooks, actually entails. It entails nothing less than a complete account of all life on earth, from its origin to the present, in strictly naturalistic terms. That being the case, there is strictly no explanatory "wiggle room" in which God can meaningfully so much as lend a hand

Mission-Centered Apologetics

in the creation. Genesis (and much related Scripture) declares that God *himself* created, as a demonstration of his own boundless power, not that God "used" some natural agent or process in a way that would render his own existence superfluous. A wholly naturalistic account of a divine miracle is a contradiction in terms. For these reasons it should be clear that evolution constitutes a major stumbling block to Christian theism.

Of course, the fact that evolution contradicts, or at least severely undermines, any defensible reading of Genesis does not mean that evolution is false. It could be that Genesis is false. However, the doubts that most people have about creationism derive not from anything inherently implausible or irrational about the prospect of God creating life on earth, but from a belief that evolution is a *fact of science*. Indeed, to hear contemporary promoters of evolutionary theory like Richard Dawkins and Jerry Coyne, evolution is not just a highly regarded theory of science – it's absolutely *true*. Dawkins asserts flatly, "Evolution is a fact. Beyond reasonable doubt, beyond serious doubt, beyond sane, informed, intelligent doubt, beyond doubt evolution is a fact."[22] The only people who seriously doubt evolution, I am often told, are religious people with prior intellectual commitments. But abundant evidence suggests that evolutionists harbor some deep intellectual commitments of their own.

Ironically, when I first began to hear scientists insist that evolution is "not just a theory," but an indisputable *fact*, is when my first real doubts about evolution began. It seemed to me that these scientists were compelled to overstate their case, almost like they were compensating for something. Thus it seems still. To hear most intellectuals today, it's cool to question just about everything, up to and including the existence of the physical world around us, in the name of intellectual inquiry. So it is that distinguished scientists like Neil deGrasse Tyson seriously entertain, and in some cases even wholly embrace, a belief that we are actually living in a computer simulation. But somehow to question *evolution* is to become a science "denier" or a kook. There is a real inconsistency here, though, because no one believes that the computer simulation we are thought to inhabit evolved by natural selection or descended from a common ancestor. Those who accept simulation theory invariably attribute the computer simulation itself to the technological and creative wizardry of aliens from an advanced civilization. (While *they* may have evolved on that theory, *we* did not.) And much like evolutionary theory itself, the computer simulation hypothesis is impossible to falsify. As philosopher David Chalmers says, "You're not going to get proof that we're not in a simulation, because any evidence that we get could be simulated."[23]

If sophisticated thinkers like Tyson and Chalmers openly question the existence of an external physical reality, which would clearly include the entire purported evolutionary history of life on earth, they certainly should be able to question evolutionary theory. The fact that they cannot bring themselves to question it therefore speaks volumes about the depth of their own intellectual commitments. The problem is that most scientific intellectuals are philosophical naturalists, and philosophical naturalism *needs* evolution, or something much like it, to be true in order to explain the biological world. The modern scientific-academic enterprise has simply invested too much into evolutionary theory to turn back now.

Reasons to Doubt Evolutionary Theory

Now again the fact that evolutionary biologists seem suspiciously overzealous about their cause does not in itself mean that evolution is false, nor even that evolution is anything less than the greatest scientific theory ever devised. Yet the question remains: *Are there reasons to doubt evolution?* To answer that, we have to first specify what we mean by *evolution* – since that term may refer to anything from the change in frequency of alleles in a population over time, which virtually no one disputes, to the belief that the entire range of biological diversity observable today descended from a common ancestor by purely natural mechanisms, which lots of people dispute. Unfortunately, when people express doubt about the second meaning of evolution, naturalists routinely castigate them for doubting the first. This somewhat slippery and often deliberately underhanded polemical tactic is known as the *fallacy of equivocation*.

Given that what people actually mean when they question evolution is almost always the second definition, the question can be rephrased: *Are there reasons to doubt that the entire range of biological diversity observable today descended from a common ancestor by purely natural mechanisms?* And the answer to *that* question is: "Yes, of course there are." For starters,

Evolution, Science and Technology

there are obvious theoretical limitations to how far a theory can be extrapolated and still be said to have empirical content – in other words, the problem of *micro-* versus *macro*evolution.

I personally don't know anyone who doubts that microevolution, or adaptive changes within species, occurs. Nor do I much doubt that isolated cases of what could be called "speciation" (one species presumably giving rise to another) occurs – though it's not mentioned nearly often enough in the literature that biologists do not actually agree on what exactly constitutes a "species."[24] Naturally, one must have a clear understanding in mind of what a species is to turn around and assert that the evolution of new species has been observed. The mistake here is in the assumption that macroevolution is just lots and lots of microevolution. That's simply not the case. Microevolution explains the ongoing adaptive development of singular, existing structures. It does not explain the origin of new structures altogether, let alone the systematic arrangement of many of those structures together in such a way that the organism could not survive apart from that very arrangement. After critically surveying various lines of purported evidence for macroevolution, biophysicist Cornelius Hunter notes, "From genetics to paleontology and other disciplines, the message is that evolution's necessary large-scale change does not appear to be a simple case of small-scale change extrapolated over time."[25]

As mentioned above, microevolution is easily observable, basically a function of natural selection, itself a function of Mendelian genetics, variation in traits, differential reproduction, and heredity. This is how a population of green and brown beetles can become a population of all brown beetles, for example. But, as I argued in a recent paper,

> ...the mechanism by which one existing variety of a species gives way to another hardly seems a sufficient mechanism for producing the sorts of large-scale structural changes that would be required to produce, in turn, the tremendous diversity of life currently observable on Earth. If extrapolated far enough [the] natural selection "algorithm" could be reasonably expected to select for *any number* of varieties and even species of beetles, yes – but only beetles. (To get beyond beetles to non-beetles, presumably, it is necessary to introduce an arbitrary quantity of mutations and selective environmental conditions in addition to the basic natural selection process...)[26]

Despite the existence of over 380,000 beetle species available for observation, and decades of research, biologists and systematists have so far failed to produce a single coherent phylogeny tracing beetle evolution.[27]

This relatively isolated (if gigantic) cluster of beetle species on the tree of life, mysteriously disconnected from its precursors, is typical of most organisms at various levels of classification, and is reflected further in the fossil record: "Being only sparingly preserved in rocks, how beetles evolved has long been a mystery, considering their overwhelming presence on the planet."[28] I don't mean to pick on beetles, but given that beetles constitute almost one-quarter of all the species of life on earth, one would think their evolutionary history would be particularly well documented. But such is not the case.

To the contrary, it's the systematically fragmentary nature of the fossil record that is well documented. For that reason we won't delve much further into it here – though it does serve as a good jumping-off point for discussing another problem of evolutionary theory, namely its resistance to falsification testing. As most any student of science (or philosophy) knows, a theory that is not at least falsifiable *in principle* is not especially rigorous scientifically. After all, the standard evolutionary excuse for direct ancestors of organisms like beetles consistently "being only sparingly preserved in the rocks" is that fossilization is such a rare event that, well, *we are lucky to have any fossils at all*. That is, the *presence* of the occasional purported common ancestor fossil *confirms* evolution, while the utter *absence* of anything like a reasonably close common ancestor fossil among countless counterexamples does not *falsify* it.

Similarly, "speciation" of bacteria and other organisms is said to confirm evolution; but that sharks and other organisms apparently have stubbornly refused to evolve for millions of years only shows that they have found a favorable "ecological niche" within the larger evolutionary scheme of things. Even the popular rhetoric of evolution seems impossible to defeat. Given that evolution entails what Darwin called "descent with modification," all biological points of similarity are presumed evidence of "descent" and all dissimilarities are evidence of "modification." But in that case every conceivable biological entity is evidence for evolution by definition. Examples of this sort of "heads I win, tails you lose" approach to the question could be multiplied.[29]

For me at least, however, the main reason for doubting evolution is that evolutionary reasoning is simply and transparently fallacious. More precisely, the logic used to explain "specifiable complexity"[30] by natural selection commits the *fallacy of composition*, "the fallacy of inferring from the fact that every part of a whole has a given property that the whole also has that property."[31] One example of the fallacy of composition would be claiming that since every person in the army can fit in a foxhole, the whole army can fit in a foxhole. Another would be an argument that because atoms are invisible, it follows that physical objects composed of atoms are equally invisible.

My inspiration for arguing that evolution is essentially a fallacy came to me while reading a transcript of a debate between evolutionary biologist Ken Miller and biochemist Michael Behe over intelligent design. Responding to Behe's argument that what he calls "irreducibly complex" systems almost certainly did not evolve by natural selection, Miller had replied that "evolution produces complex organs in a series of fully functional intermediate stages." At that point he added, "If each of the intermediate stages can be favored by natural selection, then so can the whole pathway."[32]

Now Miller's statement appears to be a textbook example of the fallacy of composition, in that what is presumed true of the parts ("can be favored by natural selection"), Miller asserts to be true of the whole *as a logical consequence*. Miller is not alone in this. As he says, Darwin first suggested it; and Dawkins and Coyne reason similarly. Thus my argument:

> 1. Evolutionary theory postulates that because natural selection explains the development of the individual structural components of a biological system, natural selection explains the development of the entire system.
>
> 2. To postulate that because the individual structural components of a system are alike in some way, the whole system is alike in the same way, is to commit the fallacy of composition.
>
> 3. Evolutionary theory is a fallacy.[33]

In other words, the inference from natural selection to the evolution of functionally complex biological systems is not logically warranted. To be fair, Miller was technically inferring the evolution of an entire *pathway* from evolution of individual "fully formed" stages within the pathway, whereas Darwin inferred evolution of the whole *structure* from evolution of components or substructures.[34] Both scenarios are certainly possible, strictly speaking; and Miller certainly would have agreed with Darwin, and vice-versa. But in either case the failure of *logic* is the same. Here it's important to recall that what distinguished Darwin was not his scientific "discovery" of natural selection, which biologists had observed for centuries, but his metaphysical thesis that natural selection was the key to explaining the origin, proliferation and diversity of all forms of life on earth.

This is my third time presenting the basic argument in print, though it's treated in most detail in my "Black Box Logic" article. To date no one has attempted a serious rebuttal. Meanwhile Dawkins, et al, continue to promulgate the clearly erroneous belief that functional complexity is best explained in terms of accumulated instances of natural selection. This is analogous to a belief that the construction of an industrial skyscraper can be best explained in terms of the accumulated individual efforts of various tradesmen – masons, steelworkers, carpenters, plumbers, electricians, etc. – all of them blind, and working without any architectural plans, engineering drawings, specifications, or supervision, let alone any stated purpose. Even if the plumber, say, somehow succeeded in building a viable, stand-alone system of sinks, faucets, pipes, fittings, etc., his system would still somehow have to be carefully integrated with all the *other* systems for anything like a functional skyscraper to emerge. Complex construction projects require careful planning, design, and well-managed, coordinated execution – all of which natural selection explicitly denies.

However, it could be argued, evolution also depends heavily on vast eons of time and countless cycles of reproduction, for which there is no suitable modern analogy. Given enough time and reproduction, it may be that natural selection can match, and even surpass, the design capabilities of human engineers. Yet regardless of how much time or reproduction we allow, the

Evolution, Science and Technology

critical distinction remains between the *origin* and the *development* of a system. Unlimited amounts of time and reproduction, along with the occasionally useful mutation, might explain *refinements* to an *existing* specifiably complex biological system, but would still not explain its origin.

Suppose that I am an expert auto mechanic, able not only to maintain and repair virtually any mechanical system, but in many cases even improve upon the original system with recently upgraded parts. It does not follow that I can design and build a new car from scratch. Design, production, maintenance and repair involve entirely different sets of skills, just as the original formation and ongoing adaptation of biological systems are two distinct sets of events.

Or consider Darwin's famous example of evolution, the beaks of the Galapagos finches. While natural selection may well explain the evolution of the finch's beak from a short and stubby variety on one island to a long and narrow variety on another, it offers no insight on the evolution of the *finch* – precisely because the finch is a functionally complex system (of functionally complex subsystems). Assuming the adequacy of natural selection to explain the elongation of the finch's beak, we are still left with no explanation for how its beak, feathers, and sense organs – not to mention nervous, digestive, circulatory, etc., systems – came together to assemble that marvelous instance of biological engineering we have come to recognize as a finch.

The practical upshot of all this is that on the explanatory logic of evolution, even if natural selection is responsible for the evolution of any number of structures in the system, the resulting function of the *overall system* is simply a coincidence. And coincidence is never an explanation.

Of the few biologists who have read my argument, none have objected to the logic of the argument itself. Most object instead on the grounds that I am not a scientist or that I am "ignorant" of the fact of evolution. (Note that neither objection would entail that evolutionary reasoning is not logically flawed.) Still, one prominent biology professor (whose career I would not want to jeopardize by naming him) was willing to go this far in a personal correspondence:

> I agree, in principle, but for many, if not most evolutionary pathways, we will never know the individual steps for sure, although we can make reasonable (and often well justified) assumptions about these steps. However, basing an argument on unknowns (or unknowables) is not very constructive….On the other hand, based on what we do know, there is simply no doubt about evolution. I often refer skeptics to the 5 million papers about evolution listed on Google Scholar…

Now I actually agree that a negative critique of an existing theory is not constructive. But the very fact that much of the theoretical reconstruction of evolutionary pathways is based on *assumptions*, as he says, suggests that the best explanation for the construction of functionally complex systems is still up for grabs – five million papers about evolution on Google Scholar notwithstanding. More to the point, an explanation that is logically fallacious on its face is arguably even less constructive than an honest confession of ignorance.

Why Scientific Theories Are Not True

Beyond everything said to this point, there are some good basic reasons to question *any* general scientific theory. In ages past this would have gone without saying; but the current fascination, and even religious reverence, for science, combined with the *political* necessity of affirming the truth of ideas like evolutionary theory and global warming/climate change, means we have to briefly review those reasons. These have to do with the *nature* of science and the *history* of science.

As mentioned before, one of the hallmarks of the scientific enterprise is that its theoretical conclusions are always tentatively drawn. Therefore even the best scientific theory remains falsifiable in principle (or at least subject to possible future revision or replacement). The trouble that evolutionists have on this point is trying to occupy an impossible middle ground in saying their theory is absolute truth, on one hand, and still falsifiable in principle, on the other. If their theory is absolutely true, it's not within the domain of science by definition. But if it's falsifiable in principle, then there is no reason why fellow scientists and others shouldn't question and criticize it. Yet neither of these positions is acceptable for scientific intellectuals, who want us to believe evolution without reservation but at the same time not be dogmatic about it. It's like a man who strives valiantly to prove himself more intelligent, successful, athletic and good-looking than all the men around him, but also wants to be considered humble. He simply can't be all these things at once.

The history of science likewise seems to discourage scientific absolutism or dogmatism. Consider the history of cosmology. For centuries the wisest, most enlightened thinkers accepted that the earth was the center of the universe. One "leading scientist" of the ancient world, Ptolemy, explained the orbits of the heavenly bodies in terms of the various paths taken by the sun, the moon, the planets and the stars in the night sky, using sophisticated mathematics. But in the sixteenth century Nicolas Copernicus demonstrated that the sun was actually at the center of the universe, rather than the earth. Four centuries or so after that, through the work of Edwin Hubble, Stephen Hawking and others, various lines of evidence confirmed the Big Bang theory, and with it, the implication that there was really no center of the universe at all.

We can easily imagine Ptolemy and the Greeks ridiculing the naïve flat-earth belief that held sway in the centuries before them. We can just as easily imagine Copernicus shaking his head at the ridiculously complicated Ptolemaic system. And many twentieth-century scientists had scant reverence for Copernicus once the evidence for the Big Bang began to mount. But what of our own cosmology in this century? Given the history preceding us, we would be unwise to pronounce ourselves gloriously enlightened and previous generations lost in darkness and ignorance.

These and similar observations have led some philosophers to propose what's called a *pessimistic meta-induction*, basically an inference from the history of

Evolution, Science and Technology

science that presently accepted scientific discoveries will likely be greatly modified, or even displaced altogether, in the future as knowledge continues to accumulate. In other words, scientific theories are not really *true* in any meaningful sense. They are merely reflections of our current interpretations of scientific evidence. And as mentioned in our analysis of evidence for the gospel, evidence is not really truth functional. Why is that? Well, to mean anything, *evidence* has to be called upon to support a certain theory. A theory in turn is based on predictions, of this form: *if theory X is true, Y will occur*. The problem is with reasoning further: *Y has occurred; therefore X is true*. In other words, the basic methodology of theoretical science commits a certain fallacy of logic known as *affirming the consequent*. That is,

If p, then q.
q.
p.

The truth of the conditional in the first premise entails only that q follows from p. It does not entail also that p follows from q. The reason p doesn't follow from q at the same time is that there are potentially an infinite number of reasons or causes for q. Consider for example the theory that a ghost is opening the doors of my house in the middle of the night, causing them to creak:

If g, then c.
c.
g.

Given that the conditional is true – that if ghosts were opening the doors in the middle of the night, the doors would indeed creak – and given that the doors do in fact creak in the middle of the night; it does not follow that ghosts are actually opening the doors in the middle of the night. The cause of the doors opening, hence creaking, could be the dog, my daughter, a thief, the wind, a demon, an angel, etc. So even if it is correct to say that if theory X is true, Y will occur, and even if Y in fact occurs, Y's occurrence is not sufficient to conclude that theory X is true. Though I suppose a given scientific theory *may* ultimately be true in some highly abstract and generalized sense, the nature of science itself means that we are not in a position to know it.[35]

The Worship of Science and Technology

Unfortunately, most of the above discussion is completely lost on recent generations, who have been led to believe that the truth of leading scientific theories, like quantum mechanics or general relativity, is every bit as self-evident as the truth that two and two equals four. I mention quantum mechanics and general relativity specifically, for a couple of reasons: (1) each is as about as well-established as a scientific theory can be; and yet at the same time, (2) each is inconsistent with the other. Or as Stephen Hawking put it bluntly: "they cannot both be correct."[36] Now if two of our best-established scientific theories cannot both be true, at least one of them is false, in which case the popular belief that leading scientific theories are always true, is also false.

Evolution, Science and Technology

Logical incompatibility notwithstanding, the contemporary captivation with science and technology seems indistinguishable from religious adoration. What I wrote many years ago in a long out-of-print book is actually, almost unbelievably, far more relevant now: "Certainly it is no exaggeration to say that modern fascination with the computer, with is mind-boggling power, its capacity to entertain, and its seeming omniscience, is something akin to religious worship."[37] This strange sort of general "technolatry" seems grounded in some of humanity's deepest, if most often misplaced and misleading, desires: especially the desires for pleasure, leisure, knowledge, and social interaction. Technology promises to deliver on all four in copious quantities. Motor vehicles, microwave ovens, electric blenders, elevators, video games, smart phones, spaceships, robots and social media, are but a few of countless examples of technologies designed to make life "better" in these various ways.

But of course, along with these useful, seemingly beneficial technologies are some not always so useful, often downright dangerous and frightening technologies – like switchblades, bazookas, nuclear weapons, spy cameras, malware, the dark web, and so on. In most cases, however, the technology seems morally neutral, but always carrying with it the potential for destruction. So despite intense political pressure to prevent certain acts of evil by prohibiting firearms, the fact is that firearms are morally neutral. As a result we accept their use among policemen and soldiers, for example, and even among the bodyguards assigned to protect the very politicians calling for the prohibition of firearms. For some people, social media like Facebook are a godsend, permitting the reuniting of families and friends, not to mention the low-cost promotion of social causes, businesses and products. For others, social media are a cause of sadness, distress, envy and jealousy, cyber-bullying, anxiety and even clinical depression. Quite a few studies suggest that on balance the effects of Facebook on the average user are seriously detrimental to psychological health.[38] Surprisingly, the more time people spend "connecting" on Facebook, the more isolated they feel themselves to be from other people. Perhaps more surprisingly still, Facebook use has proven to be positively *addictive* despite these obvious, manifold downsides.

Technology, we seem continually determined to forget, is always and only a *tool* for use at humanity's disposal. In that sense, an artificially intelligent robot belongs in the same category as a garden rake. Failure to recognize this basic fact leaves us vulnerable to all manner of spiritual deception. We considered earlier the growing belief that what appears to be the physical world around us is actually a "simulation" running on some alien civilization mainframe's hard drive. A yet more disturbing example of technological deception is belief in the "singularity," by which I mean not the old cosmological singularity that was the stuff of big bangs and black holes in Stephen Hawking's popular books, but a belief in a future state of unceasing exponential technological growth in which humanity will bow in awe and fear at the ever-evolving machines of our own devising. This is the ultimate idolatry, and appears to be taking place in some measure at the present.

Evolution, Science and Technology

The leading prophet of technological worship has to be Ray Kurzweil, Director of Engineering at Google and author of *The Singularity is Near: When Humans Transcend Biology*. According to Kurzweil,

> within several decades information-based technologies will encompass all human knowledge and proficiency, ultimately including the pattern-recognition powers, problem-solving skills, and emotional and moral intelligence of the human brain itself.... By the end of this century, the nonbiological portion of our intelligence will be trillions of trillions of times more powerful than unaided human intelligence.[39]

This "nonbiological portion of our intelligence" is information technology, the same technology that currently enables us to send email and browse the Internet. "Once a computer achieves a human level of intelligence," Kurzweil asserts, "it will necessarily soar past it." All this sounds like science fiction, and it probably is. There are all sorts of practical, economic and mathematical reasons to think that computer processing power, for example, cannot grow both exponentially and indefinitely. In fact various sources are already telling us that "Moore's Law" – the once well-founded rule that computing power will double every year – simply no longer holds.[40] What's most remarkable about the singularity thesis, however, is not its outlandish confidence in technology to overwhelm all human capabilities, but that devotees like Kurzweil believe such technology will be purely beneficial to mankind.

Mission-Centered Apologetics

Here we have a strange marriage of the most advanced yet unrestrained kind of technological power, with the most naïve, credulous kind of optimism about what it could mean for us.

While I think we should be grateful that people like Kurzweil are probably wrong, there is a biblical sense in which they may turn out to be right. For centuries scholars have struggled to properly understand and interpret passages alluding to the "Antichrist," or "the beast." Revelation describes the beast's power: "He causes all, both small and great, rich and poor, free and slave, to receive a mark on their right hand or on their foreheads, and that no one may buy or sell except one who has the mark or the name of the beast, or the number of his name" (Rev. 13:16-17). For this and other reasons, "All who dwell on the earth will worship him" (v. 8). End-times speculators, using all kinds of ingenious numerological devices, have identified the beast with Nero, Pope Leo X, Napoleon Bonaparte, Adolf Hitler, Ronald Reagan, Barack Obama, and even humanity at large. But in the context of a society openly given to technology worship, the identity of the beast may soon become much more clear. The beast may be nothing more – but nothing less – than a seemingly all-powerful, superintelligent machine.

It is certainly conceivable that in the not too distant future a centralized, secularized global government led by an artificially intelligent supercomputer will directly regulate and control all human activity, including economic transactions, thereby determining just who can and cannot buy or sell goods. Those who do not show proper deference and reverence for this supercomputer and its system – those who do not "worship the beast," so to speak – will bear its wrath.

Science and the Gospel

At the heart of the good news of the gospel is the promise of God to make a "new creation" of those who trust and obey him. But to rightly understand the concept of a "new creation," hearers of the gospel may have to first understand the original creation. This may require calling into question the entire evolutionary-scientific paradigm. When God created, he did not use existing materials and existing laws of nature. He created the materials and he created the laws. At creation God first formed chaotic matter, then ordered it systematically, and then breathed life into it (Genesis 1-2). This is an expression of transcendent, supernatural power, and therefore is not reducible to a function of "nature" – i.e., of long stretches of time, reproduction, some genetic mutations, and lots of natural selection events. Central to any reasonable theology is the understanding that God is the Creator. God is not some spiritually wise but physically powerless or indifferent third-party witness to nature's ability to create life without him. Rather, God alone has the power to work miracles, and therefore God alone has the power to create the universe and life within it – to create nature. Creation of nature itself was God's first great miracle.

After roughly 160 years of dominance by the scientific-evolutionary paradigm, it's time that evangelists and apologists begin to reclaim and reassert God's creative power in their proclamation of the gospel. A revelation of the nature-transcending, creative power of God brings with it the hope that God can work miracles at a personal level – that "the kingdom of heaven is at hand" for each of us, as individual creations. God calls weak, sinful, mortals to walk in "newness of life" by the power of his Spirit.

But he also calls us to worship him *alone*. Both testaments of Scripture declare that there is but one God; thus we are repeatedly cautioned to "flee from idolatry." In the present age, breaking free from idols often means refusing to bow before scientists, theoreticians and technocrats, and consciously choosing to worship the living God – the God of Abraham, Isaac and Jacob. According to the gospel, that same God was "made flesh" in the person of Jesus Christ, who worked miracles, exorcized demons, died for our sins, rose from the dead, and now calls all of us to repent of our sins and trust in him for salvation.

5. EXCLUSIVISM AND THE CLAIMS OF CHRIST

Today's secularized culture is marked by two distinct beliefs regarding the Christian gospel. One, reviewed in the previous chapter, is that purportedly indisputable truths of science like evolution have shown Christianity to be implausible, if not altogether falsified. The other, scarcely compatible with the first, is that Christianity cannot be true because the sheer number of competing truth claims in the world means that no individual belief can be true while the others are false. Philosopher J.P. Moreland has taken notice of this strange duplicity of thought and called it *axiological postmodernism*:

> Standing behind axiological postmodernism, at least in popular culture, is an implicit epistemology that we may call *folk empiricism*, which holds that *for any belief P, P is reasonable to believe and assert if and only if P can be and has been adequately tested with one's five senses*. Let's name this claim FE. The point of FE is to limit what we can reasonably believe and assert to what can be "appropriately" tested with the five senses, and the hard sciences are taken to be the ideal exemplars of this epistemic standpoint.[41]

To put it another way: anything and everything is questionable, *except* the findings and theories of science.

Mission-Centered Apologetics

But why should science get a pass? We have seen in earlier chapters that there are good reasons to question even well-argued and popular scientific theories. One of these reasons has to do with the difference between inductive and deductive reasoning. For most of modern intellectual history we have recognized that the conclusion of a deductive argument, like the following, is true:

All men are mortal.
Socrates is a man.
Socrates is mortal.

That's because if each of the premises in a deductively valid argument are true, then the conclusion follows necessarily. Compare that with an inductive argument such as the one below:

Every swan ever observed has been white.
All swans are white.

The conclusion to the above argument does not follow logically from the premise, but seems only to be suggested by the premise in some sort of inexact, probabilistic way. Worse, the above inference is actually false. It was thought to be true many years ago, but only until 1697, when the first black swan was discovered in Australia. The case of the black swan highlights an important point about inductive, or scientific, reasoning: no matter how seemingly strong our inductive inference, it can be falsified at any time. For that reason it is a mistake to think that inductive inferences are true, rather than merely probable.

Despite all this, somehow we have managed to completely reverse what we once recognized to be a basic understanding of science and philosophy – namely that sound inductive inferences are not *true*, but probable at best, while sound deductive inferences are in fact true. Today much of society embraces the precisely opposite view. One unfortunate consequence of this strange inversion of truth and probability is the belief that non-scientific propositions are not in any sense true. So it is thought that Christianity might be a comfort to some, a useful guide to morality for others, but it cannot be true in any meaningful sense because it's not a testable scientific theory. Again, this is simply wrongheaded.

Exclusivism, Relativism and Christianity

To "believe in" Jesus presumably means to believe that what Jesus said of himself is true.[42] Certainly Jesus made strong truth claims for himself. In various places Jesus referred to himself as the "Son of God," the "Son of Man," and the Christ, or Messiah. He called himself "the Way, the Truth, and the Life" (John 14:6). When the Pharisees challenged Jesus with an appeal to their spiritual pedigree from Abraham, Jesus offered the astonishing reply: "Before Abraham was, I am" (John 8:58). Here Jesus claims spiritual authority above that of Abraham, the very father of all the Jews. Beyond that, he implies eternal preexistence for himself, in using the same language as the Lord in his revelation

Mission-Centered Apologetics

to Moses: "I AM WHO I AM." In all four Gospels, Jesus claimed the authority to forgive sins, to heal sicknesses, and to cast out demons. At times he demonstrated authority over nature itself, walking on water and causing storms to cease. He even claimed authority over the law of Moses, calling himself "Lord of the Sabbath."

Now given the modern, or postmodern, presumption that only scientifically testable propositions can be true, Jesus cannot justifiably make such pronouncements. But we have noted previously that there are reasons to think the proposition that only scientifically testable propositions can be true, is not itself true. To the contrary, such a proposition is not scientifically testable, and therefore is strictly self-defeating. In that case it may well be that Jesus is the Truth – the only way to know God and eternal life – and all competing claims are false.

Clearly the common tendency to consider Christianity untrue because it is "unscientific" is intellectually weak. The *emotional* reaction to exclusivism (based on a moral objection), however, appears to be extremely strong, sufficient to empower contemporary multiculturalism and cultural relativism apart from reason altogether. Today it's fashionable to summarily write off all claims to truth that are not scientific as ignorance, arrogance or pretension. A secular "prophet" of sorts, Allan Bloom caught wind of this many years ago. Back in 1987 he wrote: "The relativity of truth is not a theoretical insight but a moral postulate, the condition of a free society, or so they [university students] see it." So it is that students now regard Christian believers with

Exclusivism and the Claims of Christ

the same revulsion they might have reserved for witches or monarchs in times past. "The danger they have been taught to fear from absolutism is not error but intolerance."[43]

All this leads naturally to the core question of *exclusivism*. According to Plantinga, "the exclusivist holds that the tenets or some of the tenets of one religion – Christianity, let's say – are in fact true; he adds, naturally enough, that any propositions, including other religious beliefs, that are incompatible with those beliefs are false."[44] The problem is what to make of non-Christian beliefs and religions (and the fates of millions of people devoted to them), let alone the many people who have never heard the gospel. Presumably God loves non-Christians and those in faraway lands as much as he loves Christians. There are religious and non-religious perspectives; there are theistic and non-theistic religions; and there is a large variety of theistic religions. Even within Christianity there are sects and splinter groups that hold beliefs completely at odds with one another. "Isn't it," asks Plantinga, "somehow arbitrary, or irrational, or unjustified, or unwarranted, or even oppressive and imperialistic to endorse one of these as opposed to all the others?"[45] The whole idea seems patently unfair on the face of it. Why should a man born in Qatar or some remote South American jungle be expected to embrace a gospel he's never heard?

We must remember, however, that if Christianity is *true*, then as a matter of logic it *cannot* be compatible with non-Christian beliefs. Truth is exclusive by definition; it *excludes* falsehood. So if we know that the product of three and five is fifteen, for example, then we also know that the product of three and five is *not* fourteen, or sixteen, or an infinity of other numbers. Likewise, if we know the earth is (basically) a sphere, we know at the same time that the earth is not a cube or a pyramid, or again a potential infinity of other three-dimensional configurations. There is no arrogance or intolerance involved in recognizing the exclusionary nature of truth claims.

Thus if Jesus made exclusive claims, he may well be the Truth, just as he declared. By the same principle, if relativism (or inclusivism) could in some sense be considered *true*, then it would contradict – exclude – belief systems like Christianity, and thereby commit the very sin it has been laboring to avoid. If relativism or inclusivism *cannot* be considered true, on the other hand, we are left with no reason to accept it or to refuse belief systems like Christianity.

Exclusivism and the Gospel

Suppose for a moment that among the many religions in the world, just one of them is true, so that among the many purported gods, only one actually exists. Were that to be the case, we would naturally expect that God to make himself known and to declare himself as such. The history of Israel in the Old Testament, and the history of the early church in the New, are in fact largely the visitations of the one true God upon his people. From the revelation of God to Abraham, Isaac, Jacob, Moses, and the prophets, to the coming of John the Baptist, and finally, the miracle-working ministry of

Exclusivism and the Claims of Christ

Jesus, biblical history records again and again the "divine initiative" – God going out of his way to reveal himself to people he has chosen to be his witnesses. "Hear O Israel," says Jesus, repeating the Deuteronomic formula, "the Lord your God, the Lord is one." All these revelations have found their ultimate expression in the life-changing ministry, death and resurrection of Jesus. Thus the empty tomb of Jesus and the birth of the early church attest to the revelation of the one living God. The apostles understood the implications of Jesus rising from the dead to vindicate his claims: "for there is no other name under heaven given among men by which we must be saved" (Acts 4:12).

Even if the gospel makes exclusivist claims (it does), and even if most people are confused or offended by those claims (they are), apologists and evangelists must stay on mission. To that end we must bear in mind that our "postmodernized" generation desperately needs a straightforward, uncompromising declaration of the truth. At the heart of the gospel is that *truth* has been revealed in the person of Jesus Christ. Precisely because the impossible, incoherent lie of relativism has been promulgated so aggressively and relentlessly, I believe there is a genuine hunger in people to know and understand "the truth that is in Jesus," as Paul said. One of Solomon's proverbs says that "Like cold water to a weary soul is good news from a far country" (Prov. 25:25). For many seekers wearied by the emptiness and futility of postmodernism, the message that Jesus is the Truth can be a refreshing tonic.

Finally, truth lies at the heart of the power of the gospel. The ministry of deliverance, for example, often

Mission-Centered Apologetics

involves identifying the lies of Satan that have gripped and bound people into deceptive – and often demonically powerful – thought patterns of self-loathing, codependency, addiction and the like. Knowledge of the *truth*, as Jesus said, "will set you free."

POSTSCRIPT: REVISITING PASCAL'S WAGER

Most Christian apologists are inclined, I suspect, to think that apologetics is all about knowledge. So we apologists strive to learn all we can about Scripture, science, logic, history, etc., in an effort to be sufficiently knowledgeable – and thus "equipped" – to minister effectively to an increasingly skeptical world. Important as knowledge undoubtedly is for the evangelistic undertaking, however, I think we've sold short the whole concept of *wisdom*. In Scripture, wisdom is said to begin with "the fear of God." Unfortunately, every generation from the "baby boomers" of the sixties to the latest crop of Generation Z, has been explicitly taught to question authority – up to and including the authority of God – and taught moreover that all fear is "irrational."

For contemporary intellectuals, rational decision making has been reduced to a function of probability assessments and little more. However, this seems to be an unduly restricted understanding of rationality. A rational approach would surely consider not only the probability of hypotheses being true or false, but the *consequences* that would follow from those hypotheses being true or false. There would seem to be nothing especially rational, for example, about my taking a shortcut to work by crossing a bridge high over an icy lake where the probability of its collapsing sometime within the next year is "only" .25, or moving into a neighborhood where a full 60 percent of the residents have never been mugged simply because it's close to my favorite shopping center. A good and prudent soldier does not lay down his arms whenever the probability of his survival dips below .5 in the heat of battle (indeed, he is far too busy to bother with such calculations, knowing that he maximizes his probability of survival by continuing to fight). A truly rational perspective, then, understands the difference not merely between true and false, or between probable and improbable, but between wisdom and folly.

Scholars and philosophers of religion might recognize the similarity of this line of reasoning with "Pascal's Wager," a pragmatic apologetic for faith by the great mathematician and philosopher Blaise Pascal. The idea basically runs as follows. If I believe, it costs me nothing, while it benefits me a better earthly life at the least and eternal bliss in heaven at the most. If I don't believe, it benefits me nothing, while it costs me a disappointing earthly life at the least and eternal torment in hell at worst. Critics have long complained that Pascal's Wager is too selfishly calculating to be of any real spiritual value. But an argument could be made that selfish calculation is what leads to atheism in the first place. In other words, nonbelievers don't want to "waste their lives" on religious devotion, if religious devotion may not be grounded in truth. In a sense, Pascal merely extends that same kind of cynical calculation to account for potential costs and benefits in *eternal* rather than merely earthly terms.

Even apart from any consideration of facts and evidence in support of the gospel, then, it would be

Postscript: Revisiting Pascals' Wager

rational – *wise* – for any nonbeliever to at least stop and consider the eternal costs and benefits of faith in Christ versus unbelief. The message of this book, along with thousands like it, demonstrates that indeed there *are* facts and evidence in support of the gospel – in which case the already apparently rational prospect of surrendering one's life to Jesus becomes that much more rational.

Another objection to Pascal is that faith is thought to be passive; that is, one does not *choose* to believe, but rather, belief is something that *happens* to people as they experience life. This may be true to a point, but should not be overstated. Rather than try to rephrase what I've already written on this point, I will go ahead and quote an old blog post of my own:

> The fact is, even if it's true that we can't always choose whether to believe a given proposition or worldview, we do generally choose what we *want* to believe. We strongly tend to feed those beliefs we want to affirm, and starve the beliefs we would rather repudiate. Thus an atheist who says he would really like to believe in God, but spends all his time on message boards and blogs arguing against that belief at every opportunity, is not being entirely honest. The same could be said of a Christian who complains that his faith is weak and he just can't help it, but spends little or no time in prayer or meditating on the words of Scripture. For all of us, belief has a way of aligning itself with the heart's desire and picking up where evidence leaves off.[46]

Mission-Centered Apologetics

Observing that we "do not always have the luxury of avoiding cognitive commitment until we can be sure that we have avoided cognitive error," Doug Geivett describes his "prudential" approach this way: "The sincere inquirer…should adopt a policy of inquiry that greatly improves rather than diminishes her chances of sincerely and responsibly believing in God should it be the case that God exists."[47] Wisdom gives the benefit of a doubt not only to the option which rings most true, but which holds out the greatest rewards and severest consequences – *eternal* rewards and consequences in this case. In our efforts to win souls for Jesus Christ, we must be bold to appeal to wisdom and not merely intellectual sophistication.

On one point I must disagree with Pascal: while there is much joy in finding the kingdom of God and living a life for Jesus, there is also a heavy price to pay. ("Count the cost," Jesus advised all his prospective disciples.) But the price for refusing Jesus is much heavier still. I therefore leave the last word on this topic, and the last word of this book, to Jesus Christ himself:

> "If anyone desires to come after Me, let him deny himself and follow Me. For whoever desires to save his life will lose it; but whoever loses his life for My sake will find it. For what profit is it to a man if he gains the whole world, and loses his own soul? Or what will a man give in exchange for his soul? For the Son of Man will come in the glory of His Father with his angels, and then He will reward each according to his works" (Matt. 16:24-27).

ENDNOTES

---

[1] Peter Kreeft & Ronald Tacelli, *Handbook of Christian Apologetics* (Downer's Grove, IL: Intervarsity Press, 1994), p. 48.

[2] Jane Coasten, Anna North, & Andrew Prokop, "Jeffrey Epstein, Explained," *Vox* (Sept. 4, 2019), https://www.vox.com/2018/12/3/18116351/jeffrey-epstein-case-indictment-arrested-trump-clinton.

[3] Jaclyn Gallucci, "Sex Trafficking is an Epidemic in the U.S. It's Also Big Business," *Fortune* (April 14, 2019), https://fortune.com/2019/04/14/human-sex-trafficking-us-slavery/.

[4] Dietrich Bonhoeffer, *The Cost of Discipleship*, (New York: Simon & Schuster, 1995), pp. 35-36.

[5] Naturally, the same argument could be reversed: Given the many assurances of Jesus and the apostles that genuine believers would "suffer persecution," and must "through many tribulations enter the kingdom of God," we could just as easily say that a *lack of suffering* is evidence of worldliness or unbelief.

[6] According to one scholar at least, the only known source for this now-famous "Epicurean Paradox" was actually Lactanius, a third-century Christian apologist. – Bernard Schweitzer, *Hating God: The Untold Story of Misotheism* (New York: Oxford, 2011), p. 31.

Mission-Centered Apologetics

---

[7] See Alvin Plantinga, "The Free Will Defense," from Raymond Martin & Christopher Bernard, *God Matters: Readings in the Philosophy of Religion* (New York: Longman, 2003), p. 295-314.

[8] Aurelius Augustine, *Confessions*, (Peabody, Mass: Hendrickson, 2004), p. 130.

[9] D. McIntosh, *Transcending Vision: Christian Theology in an Age of Empiricism* (Houston: Gerizim Publishing, 2018), p. 181.

[10] Michael Martin, *Atheism: A Philosophical Justification* (Philadelphia: Temple Univ. Press, 1990), p. 428-429.

[11] C. Stephen Evans & Zachary Manis, *Philosophy of Religion: Thinking About Faith* (Downer's Grove, IL: Intervarsity Press, 2009), p. 167.

[12] D. McIntosh, *Transcending Proof: In Defense of Christian Theism* (Houston: Christian Cadre), p. 22.

[13] McIntosh, *Transcending Proof*, p. 26.

[14] Cited in Chad V. Meister, *Evil: A Guide for the Perplexed*, (New York, Bloomsbury, 2018), pp 82-83.

[15] Derek Morphew, *Breakthrough: Discovering the Kingdom* (Cape Town, South Africa: Vineyard International Publishing, 2006), p. 9.

Endnotes

---

[16] William Clifford, "It Is Wrong to Believe Without Evidence," from Martin & Bernard, *God Matters*, p. 182.

[17] Some atheists disagree. See for example, Richard Carrier, "Proving a Negative," *Secular Web* (1999), https://infidels.org/library/modern/richard_carrier/theory.html. [For my rebuttal to Carrier, see D. McIntosh, "Transcending Proof," *Secular Web* (2014), https://infidels.org/library/modern/don_mcintosh/transcending-proof.html). And for Carrier's rejoinder to my rebuttal, see "Misunderstanding the Burden of Proof," *Richard Carrier Blogs* (2019), https://www.richard-carrier.info/archives/ 15029.]

[18] Antony Flew, "The Presumption of Atheism," *Canadian Journal of Philosophy*, Vol. 2, No. 1 (1972), pp. 29-46.

[19] For a more developed defense of this position, see Alvin Plantinga, *Knowledge and Christian Belief* (Grand Rapids, MI: Eerdman's, 2015).

[20] See Richard Swinburne, *The Existence of God* (New York: Oxford, 2006), p. 52-72.

[21] Jeffery Jay Lowder, "Christian philosopher says the popularity of apologetics book shows Christians care about evidence," *Secular Outpost* [blog] (2015), https://www.patheos.com/blogs/secularoutpost/ 2015/12/16/christian-philosopher-says-the-popularity-of-apologetics-book-shows-christians-care-about-evidence/#disqusthread.

[22] Richard Dawkins, *The Greatest Show on Earth: The Evidence for Evolution* (New York: The Free Press, 2009), p. 8.

[23] Cited in Clara Moskowitz, "Are We Living in a Computer Simulation?", *Scientific American* (April 7, 2016), https://www.scientificamerican.com/article/are-we-living-in-a-computer-simulation.

[24] According to one expert on the subject, there are 26 species concepts "presently in play." – John Wilkins, "A List of 26 Species 'Concepts,' *Science Blogs*, https://scienceblogs.com/evolvingthoughts/2006/10/01/a-list-of-26-species-concepts.

[25] Cornelius Hunter, "Why Evolution Fails the Test of Science," from William Dembski, ed., *Uncommon Descent: Intellectuals Who Find Darwinism Unconvincing* (Wilmington, DE: ISI Books, 2004), p. 203.

[26] D. McIntosh, "Black Box Logic: Why Evolutionary Theory is Fundamentally Flawed" (2019), https://www.academia.edu/38735629/ Black_Box_ Logic_ Why_Evolutionary_Theory_Is_Fundamentally_Flawed.

[27] Shao-Qian Zhang, Li-Heng Che, Yun Li, Dan Liang, Hong Pang, Adam Ślipiński & Peng Zhang, "Evolutionary history of Coleoptera revealed by extensive sampling of genes and species," *Nature Communications*, 9, Article 205 (2018), https://www.nature.com/articles/s41467-017-02644-4.

Endnotes

---

[28] *Wiley Earth-Pages*, "Last common ancestor of all the primates was a flying lemur" (2008), https://wileyearth-pages.wordpress.com/2008/01/01/ last-common-ancestor-of-all-the-primates-was-a-flying-lemur/.

[29] Some evolutionists have objected that the finding of a "Precambrian rabbit" or some other mammal in very ancient rocks would in fact falsify evolution. But if the countless "gaps" in the fossil record can fail to disclose vast eons of evolution, they can also conceal the existence of numerous mammals in even the earliest of the earths' history. Thus even if a Precambrian rabbit did exist, its existence would not itself be falsifiable.

[30] Or "functional complexity," or "irreducible complexity." These all mean roughly the same, in that a certain required minimum level of complexity is observed to result in a biological function upon which the organism's survival depends. Behe's now-famous example is a mousetrap: each of the parts – the base, holding bar, hammer, spring and catch – must be precisely manufactured and arranged in order for the trap to actually catch mice.

[31] "Fallacy of Composition," *Logical Fallacies*, https://www.logicalfallacies.info/relevance/composition.

[32] Ken Miller, "Answering the Biochemical Argument from Design," from Neil A. Manson, ed., *God and Design: The Teleological Argument and Modern Science* (New York: Routledge, 2003), p. 296.

[33] This is a slightly simplified version of an argument that originally went (see "Black Box Logic") as follows:

> 1. Evolution posits that the function of any complex biological system can be adequately explained as the accumulation of countless minor functional adaptations of its individual components.
>
> 2. To say that a characteristic of the whole system can be adequately explained in terms of a characteristic of its individual components is to say that a whole is equal to the sum of its parts.
>
> 3. To say that a whole is equal to the sum of its parts is to commit the fallacy of composition.
>
> 4. Evolution is a fallacy.

[34] This is essentially how Darwin explained the evolution of "Organs of Extreme Perfection and Complexity" in Chapter Six of (some editions of) the *Origin of Species*.

[35] Some would contend that *gravity* is one example of a scientific theory that is verifiably, obviously true; but that's only because of a confusion between theory and observation. Yes, it's an observable fact that objects with mass unfailingly attract. Gravity explains that fact in terms of a universal law of gravitation (Newton's theory), or a "curvature in space-time" (Einstein's). But God personally binding all objects with mass together is another theory that would explain that fact just as well. Since all these theories cannot all be true at

once, it's clear that merely explaining or predicting a fact is not sufficient to render a theory true.

[36] Stephen Hawking, *The Illustrated A Brief History of Time, Updated and Expanded Edition* (New York: Bantam Books, 1996) p. 18.

[37] D. McIntosh, *The Fall of Eutychus: And Other Good Reasons to Repent of Your Sins* (El Paso: Vantage Advertising, 1997), p. 13.

[38] See for one example, Alice G. Walton, "6 Ways Social Media Affects Our Mental Health," *Forbes* (June 30, 2017), https://www.forbes.com/sites/alicegwalton/2017/06/30/a-run-down-of-social-medias-effects-on-our-mental-health/#40b001862e5a.

[39] Ray Kurzweil, *The Singularity Is Near: When Humans Transcend Biology* (New York: Penguin, 2005), p. 8.

[40] Tom Simonite, "Moore's Law Is Dead. Now What?", *MIT Technology Review* (May 13, 2016), https://www.technologyreview.com/s/601441/moores-law-is-dead-now-what/.

[41] J. P. Moreland, "Four Degrees of Postmodernism," from Paul Copan & William Lane Craig, eds., *Come Let Us Reason: New Essays in Christian Apologetics*, B&H Academic, Nashville, 2012, p. 31.

[42] I am proceeding here on the assumption that Jesus actually existed as a person of history. For the tiny

handful of scholars, like Richard Carrier, who argue to the contrary, I will concede only this: once we call into question the obvious, the obvious admittedly becomes difficult to prove. That said, I will be happy to "prove" that Jesus existed as soon as Carrier proves that *any* person from history existed – or that conclusions of sound logical arguments are true rather than false, that we are living in the real world rather than a computer simulation, etc.

[43] Allan Bloom, *The Closing of the American Mind* (New York: Simon & Schuster, 1987), p. 25.

[44] Alvin Plantinga, "A Defense of Religious Exclusivism," from Martin & Bernard, *God Matters*, p. 511.

[45] Plantinga, "A Defense of Religious Exclusivism," p. 511.

[46] D. McIntosh, "Is Belief a Function of Evidence?", *Cadre Comments* [blog] (2107), http://christiancadre.blogspot.com/2017/05/is-belief-function-of-evidence.html.

[47] Douglas Geivett, "A Pascalian Rejoinder to the Presumption of Atheism," from Martin & Bernard, *God Matters*, p. 172.

www.ingramcontent.com/pod-product-compliance
Lightning Source LLC
Chambersburg PA
CBHW070525030426
42337CB00016B/2109